Just One More Day

A Dog Lovers Guide to Quality of Life and Healing from Pet Loss

Geoffrey Bain

ENCHANTED FOREST PRESS
enchantedforestpress.com

Just One More Day
A Dog Lovers Guide to Quality of Life and Healing from Pet Loss

First Publishing April 2012

ISBN: 978-0-9852070-4-5

Library of Congress Control Number: 2012936541

Printed in the United States of America

10 9 8 7 6 5 4 3 2 1

Art Direction, Book Design and Cover Design © 2012

All Rights Reserved by

ENCHANTED
FOREST PRESS
enchantedforestpress.com

Book design by Reflection Studios
www.reflectionstudiosonline.com

I dedicate this book to everyone who has faced
the heartbreak of saying good-bye to their best friend…

their dog.

"A wonderful book and a tribute to the amazing human-animal bond."

—Dr. Alice Villalobos, DVM, DPNAP, President, Society for Veterinary Medical Ethics.

"One of the more difficult aspects of losing a pet is the fear of loneliness. The personal stories of how others have moved through the grief of losing a beloved companion in "Just One More Day" is comforting, enlightening and a reminder that you are not alone. The book covers many aspects of losing a loved pet, so that anyone can find a passage that connects and engages them."

—Dr. Jennifer Scarlett, Co-President, San Francisco SPCA.

"Your book is a great resource for pet lover's struggling to make the right end-of-life decisions for their companions. The combination of information from doctors, therapists and other professionals, combined with first-person stories from pet lovers strikes a good balance of fact and emotion. Your book is a support group on paper."

—Laurie Shapiro, Veterinary Cancer Group

"Marvelously poignant. It affected me deeply and I intend to use it as a resource for my work on "Just Answer.com"

—Michael Salkin, DVM, bigislandvet

"Everyone with a pet should own a copy of this book in their library. I will surely recommend it to my friends and clients who are in bereavement as a must read. I am including it as a valuable resource for coping with pet loss."

—Marian Silverman, Pet Loss Grief Counselor

"This book is a compilation of warm and loving remembrances dealing with the loss of our canine friends. Sprinkled with counseling from professionals in the field of veterinary science, psychology and education, "Just One More Day—A Dog Lovers Guide to Quality of Life and Healing From Pet Loss" is a welcome guide to assist those in need of comfort during a most difficult time."

—Rivanne Chasteen-Futch, Librarian, Lakeland, FL

"There is truly no 'one size fits all' when it comes to dealing with making the decision to assist your animal to make its transition. Geoffrey Bain's book 'Just One More Day' is a beautiful and compassionate look at the various options and points of view of many who have faced this difficult time. Thank you for all the love you put into this book".

—Marcia Breitenbach, Transformation Specialist

"This is a very useful tool for someone going through the loss of a pet. Being that I work at an animal hospital and deal with this sort of thing on a daily basis, it's always painful and time is all that heals us. Abby's triumph and journey is a great story on how it truly is different for every pet with every diagnosis."

—Tracy Towne, Foothills Animal Hospital

"I got this book for my kids (Yeah right . . .) when our neighbor's dog died of cancer. It is a gem of a book, and any one story can give you the right words or perspective to ease your loved ones through the abnormally strong pain of losing a pet. It WILL bring a tear or two to your eyes, but from admiration and love of both pets and people in similar circumstances. I got sideswiped by how much this particular loss affected me, but the book helped me grieve without embarrassment and without regret, and help my children through it as well. Big thumbs up."

—Hal Christopher Salter, Piano Magic

"I loved the book. It has helped me understand how to make the decision to relieve the suffering of my current old dog. When the time comes, I'll be better prepared and less selfish."

—Roca Welch

"I read it the same evening I got it, loved it and then loaned to my neighbor, whose dog is 17 and fading fast. She also loved it and asked if her friend could read it…. It's now on round 6 and one of these days I'll see it again!"

—Marcia Kirschbaum

"I loved the book. I wish I had it to read when I lost all of my dogs. I still miss them. You did a beautiful job"

—Peggy Dlubac

"This book will inspire pet owners and give them peace after the loss of their best friend"

—Susan Santsche

"This is a most beautifully written book. It's going to be so wonderful for pet owners to reflect on the love of their babies."

—Lisa Repoli

You have written a very important book. Every pet owner should read it. I am now able to remember with fondness rather than pain. Thank you and Bless you for this book"

—Deb Smith Elliott

"Your wonderful book brought up suppressed tears as I read it, and I know it's helping me with a healing that continues".

—Jason Matthews

"Your book is beautiful! The advice you offer, and the many different viewpoints and perspectives make it very touching, and an extremely relevant book.

—Teresa Brewer

"I pray that your book circulates around the world to comfort those that are in so much pain due to a decision needing to be made or for those who have just lost a true best friend, their pet."

—Lizz Juarez

ABOUT THE AUTHOR

Geoff Bain was born in Liverpool, England and attended Liverpool Institute High School at the same time as two of the Beatles—Sir Paul McCartney and George Harrison. After some world traveling, he settled in California, and became a Real Estate Broker for thirty years. He currently resides in Southern California. The inspiration for his first book, Just One More Day, came from an uncertainty as to when it would be the right time to call the vet to say good-bye to Abby, an Australian Shepherd who had just been diagnosed with bone cancer. Abby was the first dog in Geoff's life and she left her paw-prints on his heart. This profound experience changed his life and he is now serving others through speaking engagements, book signings and teaching others how to "Heel" a broken heart. Geoff is the CEO for WagDazzle, a new line of pet products. Please go to www.JustOneMoreDayTheBook.com to view the book trailer, read the Blog, and order more books.

CONTENTS

ACKNOWLEDGMENTS

Abby—
Thank you for teaching me the awesome power of
unconditional love. I'll bring another squeaky toy with
me when I meet you on the Rainbow Bridge.

To Kris Harmon—
your creative genius brought this book to life.

To my focus group, Naja, Alexandra and Nancy—
Thanks for all the great ideas.

To Leonard Szymczak—
Thanks for your passion, for embodying the excitement of writing.

To Margot Vincent—
an English teacher at Elmwood Franklin School in Buffalo, NY,
who took the time to critique and support my endeavors.

To Clint who showered Abby with love her whole life through.

To my delectable wife, Dawn,
my best friend, my companion, my cajoler—
Thank you for all the gentle shoves, the insight,
the deadlines, the belief, the faith and the love.

INTRODUCTION

This was the day we had dreaded for nine months. Dawn cradled Abby's head in her lap as the vet pushed the plunger on the syringe. It was over so fast. She was gone.

Abby came into my life when I married my wife, Dawn. I had never had a dog of my own before. Abby was fun and she was part of my new family. She was an Australian/Queensland shepherd mix—a rescue dog that Dawn had loved since Abby was about 6 weeks old. Little did I realize how this dog would influence my life—forever. I never could have imagined how one slightly overweight dog would touch my heart so dearly. Uncertainty evolved into unconditional love, which is what Abby taught me to see, to share, to receive and to give. I even learned how to pick up poop without gagging. Miracles happen!

Early last year, we took Abby to get checked out for a limp that we thought was a pulled muscle or tendon. She was 12, and we thought that she was getting a little creaky in her joints. Abby was diagnosed with bone cancer (osteosarcoma) in her front left leg. This is an aggressive, highly malignant form of cancer. Surgery was not an option because Abby had too much weight in the front. Other treatments might prolong her life for a few months, but at the cost of quality of life. Our vet offered to put Abby to sleep right then and there, if we wanted. It was all too sudden for us to make any kind of decision at that moment. We were told we had maybe two more months, at best.

After the diagnosis, we were determined to make sure that Abby was really, really happy every single day that she had left. We bought her more squeaky toys, and fed her the food she begged for …the cat's food! I took her for car rides almost every day so she could stick her head out of the window and feel the rush of wind across her nose. It's amazing how dying makes you really want to live.

The question that was uppermost in my mind was "How do you know when it's time to put your beloved dog to sleep?" Friends told me that I would see it in Abby's eyes. I don't think I ever did. All I saw was a waggy tail and "Please give me some more cat food" looks and "Let's play more throw-the-ball" looks. The "It's time for me to go" look never came. I just saw a bigger lump on Abby's paw, indicating that the cancer was indeed spreading fast. And I saw her limp a lot more frequently, and constantly lick her paw. One afternoon, I saw her fall in the yard, and I knew that we should call the vet.

Abby left us surrounded with love. I know we did the right thing by having the vet come to our home. So often, our loved ones, our human family, want to go home to die. That's where they feel the most love. I feel strongly that our beloved pets want that too.

It's been over a year since we called the vet to come and help our beloved Abby across the Rainbow Bridge. I'm still haunted by the image in my mind of Abby lying on her bed after the injection. I'm still tormented by the un-answerable question "Did we do it too soon?" I still burst into tears looking at her photo.

Yet, I'm comforted by the sure and certain knowledge that we made our decision based on pure love for Abby. We wanted to spare her the additional pain of a broken leg and we accomplished that.

For a while, we made dog-barking sounds whenever the doorbell rang, because we missed Abby's protective bark so much. Someday, maybe soon, we'll find another dog to love. But no-one will ever replace Abby in our hearts. She was pure, unconditional love and we miss her so.

The purpose of this book was to help me heal and move through the pain of losing Abby. In doing so, I have found that it is a subject so many people suffer through, sometimes all alone. We have support when we lose a human family member. Why does it seem less significant when we lose a beloved pet? Aren't they people too?

There is no sure way to know when it's time. I searched for answers by writing to everyone I knew, asking for help. The response was overwhelming. Some of the stories are reprinted here. So many people voiced the ever-present pain from their decision. Others expressed excruciating and still lingering guilt over waiting too long to make their decision. My heartfelt desire is that you may find comfort and help within the pages of this book.

May your decision be a little easier, may the grief be lessened and may you be comforted in knowing that your beloved pet is waiting for you across the Rainbow Bridge—leaving love tugs in your heart and healthy paw prints in the sand.

In Memory of

Our Beloved Abby

October 31, 1997—November 30, 2009

We Will Always Love You

Bye For Now...

The RAINBOW BRIDGE

Author Unknown

Just this side of Heaven is a place called The Rainbow Bridge.

When an animal dies that has been especially close to someone here, that pet goes to The Rainbow Bridge. There are meadows and hills for all of our special friends so they can run and play together. There is plenty of food, water, and sunshine, and our friends are warm and comfortable.

All the animals that had been ill and old are restored to health and vigor. Those who were hurt or maimed are made whole and strong again, just as we remember them in our dreams of days and times gone by. The animals are happy and content, except for one small thing; they each miss someone very special to them, who had to be left behind.

They all run and play together, but the day comes when one suddenly stops and looks into the distance. His bright eyes are intent. His eager body quivers. Suddenly he begins to run from the group, flying over the green grass, his legs carrying him faster and faster.

You have been spotted, and when you and your special friend finally meet, you cling together in joyous reunion, never to be parted again. The happy kisses rain upon your face; your hands again caress the beloved head, and you look once more into the trusting eyes of your pet, so long gone from your life but never absent from your heart.

Then you cross The Rainbow Bridge together....

FURRY FACTS

- It is estimated that there are close to 80 million pet dogs in the U.S.

- 45 million households own at least 1 dog.

- Almost 50% of pet owners consider their pets to be a family member.

- In 6 years, one unspayed female dog and her offspring can reproduce 67,000 dogs.

- 5 out of 10 dogs in shelters are euthanized because there is no-one to adopt them.

- 20% of people who adopt a dog from a shelter return them to a shelter.

- 7 dogs and cats are born every day for each person born in the U.S. Of those, only 1 in 5 puppies and kittens stay in their original home for their natural lifetime. The remaining 4 out of 5 are abandoned in the streets or end up in a shelter.

The statistics regarding Cancer in dogs are ALARMING: Pet Cancer is on the rise.

- 60% of dogs over age 6 will develop some form of cancer.

- 50% of dogs in their senior years will die of cancer.

- In the U.S. alone, almost 1 million dogs die of cancer each year.

Dogs are...

- twice as likely as humans to develop leukemia

- 4 times as likely to develop breast cancer

- 8 times as likely to develop bone cancer

- 35 times as likely to develop skin cancer

Statistics obtained from ASPCA (aspca.org); the Humane Society of the United States; Spay USA;Pet Cancer Foundation.

How
do I
Know
it's
Time?

*The greatness of a nation and its
moral progress can be judged by the way
its animals are treated. I hold that,
the more helpless a creature,
the more entitled it is to the protection
by man from the cruelty of man.*

—*Mahatma Gandhi*

"HOW WILL I KNOW"

Emma Riley Sutton

"How will I know when THAT day has come?" I asked my veterinarian. We had been talking about my Bassett hound, Baxter. He had been diagnosed with a debilitating and painful back problem common to most hounds—the joy of having long, heavy bodies and short legs. We both knew the time was coming to end his suffering. And also, to end ours. He was fighting valiantly, but his pain was getting worse.

"Only you can answer that," she replied. She tugged gently at Baxter's ear. "You will know when it is time."

On the way home, I decided that Baxter would tell me. I didn't know how he would tell me that it was that time, but I knew he would find a way. He had a gift for communication and I was sure he would let his feelings be known. I just had to recognize his hints and signs.

I started coping with the thought of euthanasia when I first found out about his medical condition. I knew I would do all I could to help him fight. We went to all sorts of specialists. We tried medications, herbal remedies, and even vitamins. Baxter took painful injections directly into his spine daily to get his pain under control. As his pain became more manageable, those injections were reduced. My financial resources dwindled. I even sold my back-up car and dipped into my retirement fund to keep him pain-free.

How was Baxter going to tell me it was time? I watched him closely, waiting for him to let me know. We spent as much time together as possible. Thankfully, I worked from home so he wasn't alone during the day. We took car rides together and walks. I was slowly preparing myself for the inevitable. In the back of my mind, I was constantly wondering when and how Baxter would let me know his pain was too great and it was time for me to "help" him for the last time.

His walk became slower, but his tail was constantly wagging when we went for our walks. Baxter's appetite was just as it had always been. I had to keep an eye on him because he would eat anything he could reach. He would even forget to use the ramps I had set up to help him get on our bed and up the steps of the front porch. Baxter's eyes would light up when I would get his leash, or get his treats out of the pantry. I watched as he chased birds out of his backyard. Baxter was not giving me any clues it was getting close to his time for me to help him. Time marched on; I waited and kept loving him and caring for him.

Baxter had always taken his medicine so well. He never balked or complained. I didn't even have to "ball" his pills in a treat. I would hold it in my open hand and say, "Here is your feel better num-num" and he would eat it without any problems. One day, that changed. He turned his head several times as I held out my hand with his pills on them. I coaxed him softly, promising a treat afterwards. Still, he refused. Tears streaming, the pills went back in the bottle and I headed to the telephone. "He told me it was time," I heard myself say once the vet was on the line. "We are on our way."

I helped Baxter into the car. He couldn't do it himself today. I drove slowly to the vet's office. I pulled into the driveway, but didn't stop. I made a quick u-turn and headed to Dairy Queen. He and I always had an ice cream cone after he went to the vet. Today, we would go before the visit. I didn't know if he knew why there was a change in our routine, but I did. I sobbed out our order of two soft-serve ice cream cones to the voice coming from the metal box. I didn't even wait for my change after I was handed the two cones; I drove off and parked in the first spot available. Ice cream never tasted so awful. Thankfully, Baxter enjoyed his and helped me finish mine.

Working with animals for over fifteen years at that point, I knew the drill. I had participated in the euthanasia of hundreds of animals myself at the animal shelter where I had worked. I knew the procedure; I didn't just know what to expect once it was finished. I had been present every single time one of our animals had to be "helped," but each time I had a different reaction.

I knew I would be with Baxter, just as I had for all of my other pets. I had been with him for everything else and I would not leave Baxter to face this alone. I wasn't sure how I would find the strength to be with him, but I knew he could not be alone. I was not going to abandon my Baxter in his last moments.

The entire staff came to the waiting room to say their good-byes to Baxter. He was an office favorite. Hugs and kisses for both of us from everyone. "You two have been so brave," one of the teen-agers who cleaned the kennels said, hugging Baxter and shaking the paw Baxter offered him. This young man had been the one who had so gently moved Baxter when the heavy Basset couldn't get up by himself. There wasn't a dry eye in the building as Baxter and I made our way to the exam room.

Our vet and vet technician were waiting. The table was laid out just as I had expected. I remember looking at the needle. It was so ugly and mean-looking. I hated that needle, yet I loved it. That needle would end all his pain, unlike all the other needles we had subjected him to. With trembling hands, the vet picked up the needle and asked Baxter for his paw. He was sitting in my lap, all eighty pounds of him, but he still reached out his paw towards her, tail wagging.

"I can't see the vein," the vet said as she pulled the needle away from his leg. I looked up to see tears streaming down her cheeks as well. "I'm sorry. This is harder than I thought it would be."

Seconds later, Baxter was gone. The three of us broke down, sobbing and crying. There was no comforting any of us. The tech took Baxter out of my arms. We had made arrangements for her to come to my house and help dig his grave months earlier. She had volunteered to do this. She said it helped with her grieving process. She also offered to help me gather up all of his things, when I was ready for that.

Several days passed as I walked around in a daze. I had foster animals to care for, so I was busy, but I still ached deep inside. His toys were still lying about, and his leash was still hanging on the hook by the front door. The indention of his body was still on the bed, close to his ramp. I avoided that spot. I slept on the couch for several days—couldn't bring myself to sleep in our bed.

I cried and ate very little. I had to remember to turn off the alarms that went off when it was time for his medications. I found some peace caring for the other animals in my charge and writing all my thoughts and feelings down in the notebook I had kept. I was grieving and it would take time—lots of time. I had the blessing of coping with this for months before it actually happened, but it would still take time.

I called the vet tech and she stopped by after work to help me gather up Baxter's things. He had been a rescue dog, like all my other non-human family members, so I decided to take them to the shelter I had saved him from. Some of his things, I kept. His leash was put into a box, as was his "bed bed" blanket and stuffed banana squeaky toy. I took the box to the shelter, explaining each item as I handed it to the volunteer who was helping me. I didn't know her and she didn't know me, but we both cried as I told her all about Baxter and our life together.

"It is wonderful you cared enough to let us have these things," she told me. "He sounded like a great dog. These things will help other great dogs as they get ready to go to their homes."

I had no intention of looking around the shelter that day. I wasn't ready. I didn't know if I would ever be ready. As I was leaving, I heard a howl and I felt compelled to see who was calling to me. I made my way down the wire cages until I found the owner of that howl. It was a bloodhound mix puppy. Tripping over its long ears, it ran to me. Ignoring the sign that said not to open the cage door, I scooped up that puppy.

"You must be Nadia," I told her before even checking to see if she was a girl. I knew her name right away. She went home with me right away.

Nadia was not a replacement for Baxter. Nothing could ever replace him. I am still grieving and it has been over ten years since I "helped" him that last time. I still cope with the guilt and the sadness. The only thing that gives me any comfort is knowing his last few years were spent with me, not as a homeless pet. I also take comfort in that we both were loved and he knew I did all I could to make him happy and comfortable. I still have periods of time when I cry over my decision. This is one of those moments. I am still coping with losing him. I always will be.

Reprinted with permission, Emma Riley Sutton. First printed in "Helium". http://www.helium.com/users/408505/show_articles

WHEN SHOULD YOU PUT YOUR DOG DOWN?

How to make a decision you never want to make.

By Jon Katz

Jack sells antiques in upstate New York; he's a pretty upbeat guy, but when a vet diagnosed his 12-year-old black Lab, Schuyler, with cancer of the jaw and told Jack the prognosis was grim, he burst into tears, so upset he had to call his girlfriend to come drive him and the dog home. He called me later that night. Punctuated by sobs and silences, our conversation lasted nearly an hour. "I really don't know what to do," Jack said. "My friends say I should go to Penn or Cornell for chemo. My girlfriend says I should try alternative medicine, maybe something homeopathic. I can't bear to think of it. When do you put a dog down? How do you decide? I can't bear to lose him, but I don't want him to suffer."

We spoke three or four times over the next couple of weeks, Jack agonizing over the many options he was hearing about. The vet had urged him to euthanize the dog before Schuyler's condition worsened, but Jack had clearly decided against that. He was apparently going to put the dog down "when he was ready," and thought he wasn't ready yet. One evening, he said he'd talked to a friend and dog lover who'd told him that Schuyler would tell him when it was time to go, that Jack should watch and listen to the dog for cues. He asked if I thought this was the right course.

To be honest, I couldn't quite say what I was thinking. Each decision about the death of a dog is personal and different, dependent on context and circumstances. But if I had told him what I was thinking, it would have been this: Dogs are voiceless. They can't tell us when it's time to die, even if they were capable of such abstract thought. That's something we have to decide for them, wielding our love, compassion, and common sense as best we can.

I didn't look to my wonderful yellow Labs to tell me when it was time for them to go, one diagnosed with congestive heart failure, the other with colon cancer. The responsibility and decision, it seemed to me, was mine, not theirs. I put them down before they endured any prolonged suffering—my own choice, not a recommendation for others. In the context of the most personal decision any dog owner ever makes, there are few universal truths. Jack ended up keeping Schuyler alive for two months, until the dog's jaw had swollen to grapefruit size. When he called me again, I told him it seemed time, and he put the dog to sleep. Later, he called this the most wrenching period of his life, so painful he'd decided never to get another dog. I told him that was a shame.

It is the nature of dogs to live much shorter lives than ours—just eight years, on average—and it has always been my belief that to love and own a dog is to understand and accept that along with loyalty, love, and devotion come the ever-present specters of grief and loss. This is as integral a part of the dog-loving experience as going for walks.

There's no Idiot's Guide for this question, no handbook. The many points of view are strongly held. One vet I know says a dog should be euthanized "when it can no longer live the life of a dog—and only the owner knows when that really is." A breeder says she puts her dogs down when "their suffering exceeds their ability to take pleasure in life." A trainer I respect believes her dog should live as long as it can eat.

Another friend and dog lover says she always knows when it's time: "when the soul goes out of their eyes."

I'm not among those who believe dogs have souls, but I know what she means. There is a certain visceral "dogness" about dogs, an interest in people, food, squirrels, passing trucks—whatever—that's part of their individual spirits. When that disappears, it does seem the "soul" of the dog is gone.

But I know other owners—a growing number, according to vets—who fight to keep their dogs alive as long as possible, at all costs.

Researching my last book, I visited an emergency-care clinic that had six dogs on respirators at a cost of nearly a $1,000 per week per dog.

Their owners, the vets said, simply could not bear to lose them. In the context of America's growing love affair with dogs—there are nearly 70 million owned dogs in the United States and nearly 10 million more in shelters—this seems to me a travesty, not only for the dogs but for the humans who've lost sight of the fact that these amazing creatures are animals.

Increasingly, we've come to see our dogs as human, childlike members of our families, companions that sometimes provide us with more emotional support than friends or spouses, more satisfaction than work, more support than we can find elsewhere. As a result, people are increasingly devastated by the loss of their dogs; more uncertain about how and when to put them down, more inclined to spend thousands of dollars on surgery, alternative cures, foods, and treatments that might prolong their lives.

As the owner of three dogs, I spend more than I can truly afford to keep them healthy and vigorous. But as my conversations with Jack reminded me, they are not people. Their lives and deaths ought not be conflated or confused with human losses.

To love dogs is to know death and to accept that there's never a time we are more morally obliged to speak for them than when they face the end of their lives.

First published in Slate magazine. Reprinted with permission-Jon Katz.

*The bond with a true dog is as lasting
as the ties of this earth will ever be.*

—Konrad Lorenz

WHEN AN ANIMAL LOVED ONE DIES

By Katie Boland

In the summer of 1997, my entire pet family left for heaven. The first to go was nine year old Rosie, the Brittany I had rescued some five years earlier. She had eaten raw sewage when the pipes backed up and burst, and she was so ill, I had to put her down. I had faced mountainous vet bills her entire life for thyroid, incontinence, allergy and digestive problems. I felt guilty that I had not bonded with her like I had with the others. She was hard to love because she ate poop in the backyard and I couldn't kiss her. She gagged constantly. (Wouldn't you?)

Two days later, my dear 18 year old Siamese, Sasha, had a stroke and his kidneys failed. He was deaf and senile, having spent a good deal of his final year sitting on a (formerly) white chair, shrieking and screeching at the living room wall while vomiting intermittently. He would have died on his own within days, but I saw no reason to prolong his life and made another trip to the vet. As shaken and sad as I was, I consoled myself with the fact he'd had a wonderful, long journey and had not suffered at all. He looked like a kitten in repose.

Less than three months later, it was time to help my cherished and adored Weimaraner, Alex, leave this earth. For two years, his back end had been deteriorating. I had always said that when he was incontinent, that would be it for me. But when he was, I wasn't ready. Sometimes, Alex could still stagger outside to relieve himself, but his legs would collapse and he would fall in his poop and I'd have to clean him up. One day after returning from the vet, I placed him gently on the driveway while I locked up the car. I turned to catch him rolling down the hill, looking frightened and helpless. I knew it was time to let this mighty dog, who had been so proud in life, go on. And yet, I wasn't ready to let him go. And he would need my help to leave.

I had my own live, call-in talk radio show here in LA at the time, and I did several shows looking for answers on letting go. Not everyone agreed it was time. When I told of Alex's plight, one listener suggested wheeling him around in a wagon. That smacked of selfishness. Would he want to be dragged around like that? This once regal, powerful, incredibly fast dog? My instincts told me no. I kept wishing he'd die on his own. I hated having to decide. Looking back, I am most glad that I was with him; that he died in my daughter's and my arms; that our faces were the last ones he saw. Animals sometimes need our help to leave

My radio callers had told me to celebrate his impending passing, so we had a farewell party. Our friends all came to bid him Godspeed and we fed him filet mignon. The next day, one of my girlfriends arrived with a Whopper for his last meal. He gobbled it gratefully as I spooned with him on my bed. We took pictures and prayed and sang to him. We lit candles and played my daughter's birth music (my friend calls it "soul-traveling" music) and waited for the vet. Alex started to tremble. The vet was mercifully swift. Alex simply laid his head down in my lap and was gone. I stayed by his side until the people from the crematorium came for his body. Then I broke out the vodka and peanut M&M's.

Alex's ashes are still on my nightstand. I made an altar with candles on the spot where he used to sleep, with his obedience trophies and photos, and the collars from all three animals. It was comforting to think of them all together. But the house was deathly silent.

The pain was sharp and raw. I swore I could hear his tags jingling. I could hear all their tags. I saw wisps of Alex turning a corner. I felt his presence constantly and longed to touch him one last time. We had taken lots of pictures that we framed and placed all over the house. We had made a video. We had even kept some fur when he was shedding that last summer. I used to put my face in that fur, hoping for one last whiff, before all scent of him faded away. I felt gypped because he had lasted only eleven years. He had been the hardest dog to raise: stubborn and willful and really hyper. But he was my Boo Boo. I felt afraid without my watchdog. As a single mom, I had never feared with him around. His menacing looks belied his sweet heart.

People said, "It's only a dog." Well, I lost my youngest brother, Robert, to muscular dystrophy and Alex's loss felt the same. There was no difference. My daughter didn't feel the loss like I did. After awhile, when I would cry, she would become exasperated with me. I had to find other "pet" people, who understood, with whom I could wail. I just needed to talk about my dog. Now my daughter and I reminisce, which I can do mostly without tears, and we regale each other with stories.

Animals teach us many lessons. Their deaths gave me some perspective on the fretting we all do about our shapes. I have realized that the body is only a shell, a container for the soul. If you've ever seen a dead body of any kind, you know it is empty without spirit. Losing an animal makes you spiritual in a hurry. That shift is a great example of pain causing growth. That's why pain is a gift. Our animals continue to give to us, even as they cease to live. I also felt that watching me care for the elderly animals, and seeing me make adjustments in our lives as they aged, enriched my daughter immeasurably.

I was so bereft after Alex's death that my therapist gave me a tape called "ANIMAL DEATH, A Spiritual Journey," by Penelope Smith, an Animal Specialist. She communicates with animals telepathically, both living and dead, and counsels owners to assist them toward a more ideal relationship with their animals. She also performs grief counseling for those whose animals have left the earth. Now, for some of you, this may seem a bit out there, but if you are wallowing in sorrow and desperate for relief, you may find you are open to things you never before considered.

I wept away my grief to the sound of Smith's soothing voice. Although I was overwhelmed at times, I knew I wasn't stuck; I was moving, however slowly, through the worst of it.

In her book, "ANIMALS: our return to wholeness," Smith writes, "Loss is the tearing from that which you are so in love. Staying in the loss is hell. Coming through the pain brings a compassion so deep and rapture so ardent, you know it can only be won by the contrast—going through the depths to feel the heights." As I tried going forward, the stabs of grief and their forcefulness often surprised me, even several months later. But as they came less and less frequently, I knew I was beginning to heal.

I asked Smith for ways to ease the pain of grieving. She stresses the importance of accepting your feelings. "Don't try to rush the process. Don't deny your feelings. Don't minimize them. Love is love. Grief is grief." No matter for whom it is felt. She reminds us that animals are not lesser beings. We are all spiritual beings with form and purpose. She also recommends getting into a support group. You can meet with others who are struggling with their pets' deaths and it will normalize your own feelings. I had a male friend who confessed in bewildered amazement that he'd gone into therapy after his dog died. He had survived his divorce and relatives' deaths, but losing his beloved Claude had driven him to the therapist's couch. I know from experience that it's not healthy to let the grief accumulate inside you. It will find a way out in the form of physical aches or illnesses if left unexpressed.

When I spoke with Smith, I was eager for her to reveal ways to contact animals that have departed. She encourages making contact, saying, "Animals are spiritual beings. They love to communicate; most communications reveal their joy, love of life, patience, and generally refreshing perceptions."

Sit in a quiet place. Visualize your animal. See them as they were in life. Tell them you would like to feel them, to communicate with them. Tell them you are hurting, you are open, and you want to be in touch. You may not feel them right away. There are lots of ways to be contacted. You may be washing dishes later and you'll know they are right beside you. Or you'll hear them scratch at the door. If you invite them, they will make their presence felt. Often they visit in dreams, as do living animals, because we are most accessible during those times. When you awake, trust what you get and ask what you are supposed to learn from it.

Sasha and Rosie come and go in my dreams, reassuring me they are happy and carefree and whole. Alex comes with them, he comes alone, and he comes with other Weimaraner pals. He visits often. At Christmas, they all showed up with golden halos, howling and singing and flying around, showing off their wings and airborne abilities. Sometimes my brother Robert runs with them, freed at last from his wheelchair in life.

About a year after the deaths, while I was rebuilding my pet family, I had a dream about a little female cat that needed saving. So strong was the pull, I got up the next morning and headed straight for the pound. There she was, a fluffy little Siamese-mix kitten, pushing her paws through the cage to touch me. I felt an instant connection to her and knew she was meant to be mine. My daughter named her Phoebe. Smith talks of her being beckoned to pet stores and finding an animal that was calling to her. She tells of the lizard that literally hopped in the box to go home with her when his cage was opened. Animals have their own life path and spiritual course, just like we do. Smith explains, "Some animals don't want to be saved. Dying gets complicated for domesticated animals when they or their people do not want to let go of their life together. They may feel obligated to stay in their worn-out or mal-functioning bodies for their people's sake." She advises seeking the best treatment, then being ready to let go. We grapple today with whether or not to extend human life at all costs. Many people have "Do-Not-Resuscitate" orders for themselves, yet cannot do the same for their animals. Sometimes the most loving thing you can do is to let them go.

Often a family's first encounter with death is that of a pet's. Animals teach us how to deal with life's passing. I believe my animals died in the order they did to help me manage the grieving process, and I am very grateful to them for their wisdom and sacrifice.

Smith also talks about people who feel they've let their animals down because they weren't with them at the exact moment they left this world. She feels that some can't leave while their humans are hovering, and they need space to pass on. "It is very common for animals, like people, to die when everyone leaves them alone," Smith says. According to her, it's not unusual for some animals to die in order to follow their person to the other side. I am reminded of a friend who lost his wife to cancer and within three months of her death, their dog and two cats died too.

Some people will be ready to get a new animal right away; others may need a lot more recovery time before they are willing to risk their hearts again. Some may feel disloyal for "replacing" the pet that died. I knew I needed to fill my empty arms immediately, but I questioned getting another dog since Alex's loss had been so profound. I've heard many pet owners proclaim they'd never love another pet the way they had loved the one they'd lost.

Since I had sold my home and was living in a place with no yard, a dog was temporarily out of the question. And so my daughter and I began our new family with two Siamese kitten cousins, Willyum and Shadow, in addition to Phoebe. Having these new little beings to love was very healing. Still I longed for a dog. I couldn't pass one on the street without stopping. And so, as soon as I could, I moved us again into a house and we got our beautiful Vizsla puppy named Cecil.

Cecil picked my daughter and me. When we went to see the puppies, which were just two weeks old, this little guy wiggled out of the heap, his eyes still closed, and wobbled toward us. He reached out with his tiny paw until he found our fingers. He came running to us each week that we visited him, until we could bring him home. He knew we were his. Now I have velvet ears to kiss and puppy fur to sniff again. He reminds me of Alex every day. For awhile, my daughter was convinced he was Alex. She would look at the new animals wondering if the old ones were somehow inside them. Smith feels that many companion animals do, in fact, return to their people. Some within weeks, others take years. I asked her how one would know if an animal has reincarnated and she said the new pet would show signs, like imitating habits or demonstrating preferences of the former pet. You may think an animal has come back, but he could be a new soul who is a lot like the one you lost, who has been sent to help you in the same way his predecessor did. "Wait and trust. The universe will provide," affirms Smith.

Part of the inherent contract we make with our animals is that we will take care of them and they will predecease us. Once I experienced the death of my pets, I realized I could survive it. As painful as it was, I knew I could endure it again. That freedom in knowing releases me to welcome new pets and receive all the joy their new lives bring. Smith offers hope to those of you whose grief is lingering; "Death is not the end. It is the change from one realm and form of life to another." Amen.

I REMEMBER

by Teresa Brewer

I remember when he was born. It was a crisp March morning that promised spring would be upon us soon. We'd just gotten to work when we found her—a Beagle with terribly sprung ribs and eight precious little ones. He was still wet when he caught my eye: a robust little boy, with little flap ears and a sprinkling of white hairs on each tiny paw and at the tip of his tail.

I remember the stuffed tiger I gave him as his first toy. It was about his size, a cheap little carnival favor, but it was something he could snuggle with when he missed his momma and siblings. I didn't know I was setting a precedent. He wouldn't play with just any stuffed toy after that—it had to be a tiger.

I remember when he woke me up in the middle of the night for the first time. He was in such a hurry to get outside that he didn't wait for me and started down the stairs on his own. In his rush he went down the last few steps bouncing on his front feet as his rump balanced precariously overhead. I'm not sure how he kept from toppling over. We were so close—but the cold tile in front of the door was too much, and he didn't make it outside. It was the first time I praised a puppy for having an accident in the house—he was trying so hard!

I remember the moment I realized he wasn't going to be a small dog. He was 3 months old, and already bigger than his mother had been.

We scheduled obedience lessons and passed with flying colors. Everyone thought he was beautiful, and no one ever guessed what he was! From his spotted tongue and full double coat, we guessed his daddy was at least part Chow-Chow. My father dubbed him a "Cheagle," and he grew to a gorgeous seventy-pound dog.

I remember the first time he decided to investigate one of those pesky black "cats" with that peculiar white stripe down the back. A friend was over and we were watching a movie. There was a scuffle on the front porch. He must've gotten sprayed point-blank, because you could see the mist on his face. The stench was so strong it nearly gagged me when I opened the door. His eyes were watering, and he was foaming at the mouth as he tried to spit out the taste. Yes, a friend will help you take care of your animals. But a true friend will join you in a mad dash to Wal-Mart to get a cart full of tomato juice, then help you bathe your dog outside at midnight... in March!

I remember another time he woke me in the middle of the night. He was barking like crazy and charging into the side of my bed, literally jarring me awake. I was so disoriented. I started to get angry. He was five now and didn't have to go out in the middle of the night anymore and I was so tired. I just wanted to go back to sleep. He wouldn't let me. He practically herded me into the hallway. Halfway to the kitchen, I realized I couldn't feel my hands or feet. A single, frightened, coherent thought registered and I fumbled with my sugar meter. Newly diagnosed with diabetes, I was still learning the ropes of this dangerous disease. After a glass of juice, I was finally able to get my test strips open. My sugar was so low my meter didn't register a number. I should have called 9-1-1, but wasn't thinking clearly enough to realize it. After a couple more glasses of juice and a peanut butter sandwich, I was starting to feel better and wondered where he was. I still thought he had to go potty. I found him curled up asleep by my nightstand. He'd done what he had intended. It was the first of many times he alerted me to low blood sugar reactions.

I remember the sadness when I realized he was starting to show his age. He was nine and the few white hairs sprinkling his toes and tip of his tail were joined by many more. What joy when we found a good senior formula dog food and a quality joint supplement! The spring in his step came back, and the combination let us outrun Father Time for five more years.

I remember the morning I watched in horror as he nearly fell. He couldn't climb the four steps onto the deck anymore. Father Time's slow steady march was catching up to us. I fashioned a ramp out of a few 2 x 10s and covered it with leftover shingles for traction. He didn't like the ramp at first, but quickly got used to it. A trip to the vet the following weekend got us a prescription for some arthritis medication, and we bartered a few more slow but comfortable years.

I remember the moment I knew it was time. It felt like someone had ripped out my heart, but I knew what I had to do. He'd given me too much joy to let him suffer. I called my mother for help because I knew I couldn't lift him into my truck by myself, not without hurting him. My mother offered to drive because she knew I wouldn't be able to see the road through my tears. A midnight trip to the ER Clinic brought him peace.

I'd forgotten how much it hurts to say goodbye.

Teresa says: "This is a tribute to my dog, Bear, who I had to euthanize right before Memorial Weekend. He wasn't my first, or only, dog, but he certainly was my 'fur angel.' When I spoke with my doctor following the low blood sugar episode, I was told he had literally saved my life. We celebrated Bear's 16th birthday in March. My Rottie, Sasha, stood watch over him when I called my mother that final night, and carries his tiger around whenever she's lonely."

WHEN IT'S TIME
TO PUT YOUR DOG TO SLEEP

By Charlotte Howard

I have had dogs as pets, but when it came to the decision to have them put to sleep I was too young, and it was my parents who signed the paper and held their paws as the needle slipped under their skin. As a veterinary nurse, I have had to help owners make that awful decision to let their dog go. It is never an easy decision to make. As a professional, you need to be able to distance yourself, but it is not always possible. There have been a couple of occasions when a long-term patient has come in, too ill to continue with life. The owners have wanted to do what's best for their beloved pet, but still hurting as they make that decision. I am going to tell you a story about a dog that came into a surgery and the decision to put him to sleep.

'Danny' was a Springer Spaniel with a lot of different medical problems, but the one we were all concerned about, and knew would eventually kill him, was cancer. He was only four years old, but he was a regular within our surgery. All of the vets and nurses knew him. He even came to stay with us when his owners went on holiday, as he was too sick to stay in the kennels. He came in for regular x-rays, operations if needed, chemotherapy injections and blood tests.

One day, we got an emergency phone call from his owner. Danny had more or less collapsed. He was rushed to us, and when he arrived, he had done a complete U-turn! He was his bouncy, normal self. However, the vet on call listened to his heart, took some blood and put him in a kennel whilst we waited for the results. His white blood cell count was through the roof. He had a massive infection. We put him on an intravenous (IV) drip to boost his fluid levels and started a major antibiotic course. An x-ray showed that a mass had returned. It had attached itself to his liver. The vet wanted to operate, but there was a high risk that Danny would die on the table. If he did survive, it was not guaranteed that we would be able to remove the lump or stop it from returning.

The owners sat in the waiting room, comforted by the receptionist whilst we tried to make a list of options for them. Sadly, we knew what was top of our list, and what they would decide. I showed them into the consultation room. The vet showed them the x-ray and what we had found. Before the vet even had time to tell them their options, Danny's Mum and Dad knew what was best for him. I went to the kennel area, took out the drip, and put on his lead. I could feel the tears welling up as I led him to the consultation room. On seeing his Mum and Dad, Danny began to bounce, his tail wagging, as though there was nothing wrong. His owners hugged him before the vet and I lifted him onto the table. I held him still, his Mum stroking his head, his Dad stroking his back, as the vet drew up the pentobarbital, an agent used for euthanasia. Danny didn't even flinch as the needle slid under his skin. As the drug took effect, he simply began to flop, falling into a deep sleep. We were all crying as he took his last breath.

Putting such a young and seemingly healthy dog to sleep was the worst thing I have ever had to do as a veterinary nurse. We had all grown attached to Danny, but although he was bouncy and happy, he was very ill. Had we not put him to sleep that day, he may have collapsed again, begun to seizure and died anyway. The tumor had started to take over his body. He would not have had long left.

As a loving and caring owner, you will always feel awful as you sign away your dog's life, but hopefully you will also get some comfort in knowing that what you are doing is the best and kindest thing you can do. Imagine whether you would want to suffer in their situation or whether you would thank someone for helping you drift into an eternal sleep.

THE BIRTH OF A BOOK

Geoff Bain

Our Vet told us that Abby had probably two more months before her cancer would be out of control. After four months, I sent out an e-mail to as many people as I could, asking them how they knew it was time, what signs did they notice, what did their pets tell them, if anything.

The following stories came in response, and have been chosen for their diversity and also, in most cases, their ability to make me cry. One made me laugh.

My goal in life is to be as good of a person as my dog already thinks I am.

—*Unknown*

OUR DAISY DOG

Peggy T

I have had to come to grips with "the decision" to put my dog down on more than one occasion, but the most poignant of those times related to my 18 year old dog Daisy.

Daisy did not have a disease, but was simply old; not an offense that warranted departure from our family, but as age will do, it slowed her down a lot with a few aches, pains and limps. I could see that the muscles in her leg were at the stage of atrophy (she was part German Shepherd and part Husky) and toward the end, I did carry her out to our large yard to bask in the sun and do her "duty." But for the climbing up and down the stairs, she still maintained well.

I knew that the end would be coming soon, but with my middle child away at college, I wanted to keep her long enough for him to come home and say good-bye—which would have been the Thanksgiving holiday. One day, I did my usual placement of the dog in the backyard—a huge area surrounded by woods—and left her in the beautiful fall New England sun. An hour or so later, I went to get her to return to the house and she was gone! I knew she could not have gone far—she could barely walk, yet she was nowhere to be found. If I did not know any better, I would have thought an alien ship had abducted her.

With the help of my youngest son, we searched the area and could not find any trace of her. I had heard tales of dogs going into the woods to die, and I feared that had been her fate. For three days we searched the surrounding woods, but to no avail. When I heard that the weather was going to take a turn for the worse, I sent my son and a friend to look again. They went deeper into the woods and jumped across a ditch to go in further, though they realized that in her condition, the chances of her getting to this area were really slim. As they returned to jump over the ditch again, they found her down inside, lying upright, chest deep in water. They came back to the house and got a sheet, which they lifted her in and brought her home.

She had leaves stuck to her fur and was shivering, but other than being hungry, she was no worse for the wear. I put blankets in the dryer to wrap her for warmth, and fed her scrambled eggs. It was then that she raised her eyes and looked at me saying "I don't want to do this anymore". Through all my months of wondering when the time was right, there was absolutely no question that now the time had come.

I called one of my friends and asked that her husband come at some point to dig a hole in the back yard where the woods began, to prepare a place for her. My only request was that when it was completed, they call and let me know—I did not want to see it happen. Across the street lived my veterinarian who was also a friend and neighbor, and I called to schedule the day for her to come. She had known Daisy since she was 6 months old and had stitched her when she got hit by a car, nursed her to health from heartworm, and removed a benign breast tumor, in addition to the annual shots and check-ups.

My youngest son was 6 months old when we got Daisy, and she was his inseparable companion. Even though he was now 17, she still hovered over him like she did when he was a child. She protected him at the sidebars, lying beside it while he played, ate the crumbs that fell from his highchair, ran to fetch the Frisbee when he got old enough to throw it, and slept near him each night.

The night before Daisy left us, I lay with her on the floor looking into her eyes, stroking her and thanking her out loud for all of her faithful service. When she was three, I divorced and remained single throughout the years. She was my protector, and when she was at ease, then I knew all was well. It was because of her that I had restful nights. The next day came and Helen, the vet, was at the house to administer the drug. Because of her past experiences, whenever she saw Helen she would shake and lower her eyes, knowing that something unpleasant would most probably happen. This time was different.

I had placed her on a sheet in the kitchen. She was lying upright when Helen came in and as Helen gently spoke to her, she lay down and stretched out her paw as though she knew. I could see peace and resignation in her eyes—she was ready. Helen asked me if I was ready. I nodded. She then proceeded to inject the drug into the vein in her leg. For some reason, I was expecting a deep breath or gasp, but Daisy simply closed her eyes and slept. I remember thinking that in the middle of all this sadness, what a beautiful moment it was—that I was there for her this time—that I was helping her through this transition, after all the years that she helped me through mine.

My son did not want to be present for this, so he waited in his room. I called to tell him it was over, and after I wrapped her in the sheet, he came to carry her to her resting place in the backyard. As I followed him out to her grave, I cried many tears as the memories flooded through my mind of all that she had done for us. Here was this boy who was a baby when she started protecting him at the sandbox and now, at over 6 ft. tall, it was he who was carrying her at the end of her life. She was such an important part of our family, and now it was time to say good-bye.

David gently placed her in the hole and we covered her with the same earth that she had run on when she chased the birds, ran after the children, and fetched the balls and Frisbees. It was fitting that she should rest in the same place that she brought so much life to.

(My other son and daughter were away at school and I had called to let them know what I was doing; that Daisy had basically made the decision and I could no longer wait. I feared that she would go into the woods again, and I did not want that to be the way that she left. They understood perfectly.)

It has been about 15 years since we said good-bye. Our lives have changed and we have moved on, but the memories that she gave us still seem so vivid and fresh. She saw me through my divorce, watched 2 children go off to college, helped mother orphan kitties when their mother died, and saw us through the important as well as mundane things in life....all without complaint, and with all the loyalty and enthusiasm that God has ever granted an animal.

There were many other pets that graced our lives, and all were special in their own right—but Daisy was the first. She remained with us the longest, so it is with her that we have that special bond. She was the love of our lives. Looking back, I probably could or should have made the decision earlier—especially when I think that she could have died in the woods, all alone. But things happen the way they were intended, and I was able to see it in her eyes that day we found her.

I really loved that dog.

TRUE LOVE NEVER DIES

Emily J

My dog Jesse suffered from liver disease. We were with her during the last months when her health deteriorated dramatically. I even carried her to work so that she could rest in my office. When we saw that she was in so much pain (seen by us in her gentle eyes), we let the doctor give her the shot. We held her tightly, singing her favorite song and telling her we loved her very much. The only silver lining to this whole experience is the faith I have that I will see her again after I have to go. For true love never dies, no?

Dogs are our link to paradise.
They don't know evil or jealousy or discontent.
To sit with a dog on a hillside on a
glorious afternoon is to be back in Eden,
where doing nothing was not boring—
it was peace.

—Milan Kundera

WONDERFUL WICKETT

Dan & Mira R

This is a short story about our wonderful pet and companion 'Wickett' who was with us a good ten years before I had to put him to sleep.

I was remodeling a kitchen for a customer who had several White Highland Terriers of her own. She happened to have a good friend who owned a purebred White Highland Terrier from England, which they brought with them when they came to the United States. Due to unforeseen circumstances, they decided to return to England. They didn't want to pay the enormous quarantine fees to reintroduce the dog to England, so they decided to find a loving home for him.

Well...I asked if we could adopt him, and they soon came to our home to 'interview' the prospective owners. My wife fell in love with the dog, and the dog made itself very comfortable in our loving home. He had it made because there were no children to compete with, so he was the center of attention and absolutely adored it. It was soon apparent that it was 'Wickett' that allowed us to live here in our home with him.

Ten wonderful years went by and we could tell that age was catching up with him. He was already five years old when he came to live with us. His breathing became labored whenever we walked around the neighborhood. Because of that, we didn't walk him too much. The vet told us that his lungs couldn't absorb oxygen fast enough if he became worked up.

Well, we learned to become very aware of his breathing, and a good relaxing belly rub would be all he needed to relax. Despite our care, his breathing got worse and he was constantly laboring to catch enough air. On our last trip to the vet, it was painfully obvious that this couldn't go on. Mira couldn't come to grips with having to make the decision, because she thought Wickett would get over it. But I could see in his eyes that Wickett needed to be at rest. The unpleasant sounds of his labored breathing became too much to bear, and as we met the Vet for the last time, I told her to administer the sedative.

I'll never forget the look in his eyes as he came to understand what he was going through. As Wickett became relaxed and calm, he reached his paw over to my hand and closed his eyes as he fell asleep. I knew right away that I made the right decision for Wickett, but that didn't stop the tears from flowing from my eyes. Wickett was a loving companion and true friend.

I'm more convinced than ever that the decision can only be made with a heart full of compassion and Love for our four-legged 'family members'. And only Love can help one to understand that such a decision is the right one to make.

We miss our beloved friend 'Wickett'. But his memory is constantly making us laugh and smile.

MY ABBY DABBY GIRL

Dawn B

There she was—sleeping under a large tree with two siblings beside her. A young girl sat beside them with a sign "Puppies for Sale". Who can resist puppies? I knew better than to go over there for a quick peek. If I did, I would go home with one of those puppies. And besides, it was Christmas Eve and a puppy peek would help ease my broken heart from my Dad's recent death. Well, the magic began. As soon as I walked over there, this little, round, dirty puppy—half Australian Shepherd, half Queensland Shepherd—threw open her eyes and jumped on top of my feet...she was so excited! It was as if I was her long lost friend that she hadn't seen in years! And the other puppies were still sound asleep. So, that was it...we had found each other, and she was going home with me right then. I asked the girl how much for the puppies and she said, " My Dad said I had to come back with $60.00 or he would put them all to sleep tomorrow." I gave her $100.00 and said, "Now, please change your sign to FREE puppies".

I held her in my arms on the way home...and she instantly owned my heart. Can you imagine the joy my son experienced as I pulled this wiggly little fur ball out from under my jacket on Christmas Eve? It was my best Christmas ever. What a great surprise...for both of us! Abby was inseparable from us from that day forward. Wherever we went, Abby went...except when I went to work and my son went to school. She loved and missed us so much, and she shared how much. For a month when I came back from work, and she had chewed one of my shoes...and a different shoe each week. I never understood how she got to my shoes in the first place and why only mine? It was a small price to pay for unconditional love...and she was the sole recipient of our unconditional love for 4 years. Then it happened. We brought home a kitten. This was another "please take me home" experience…come to Dawn's house, the home of soft hearts and lots of love. Well, this kitty turned out to be a Maine Coon Cat…and soon to be Abby's new best friend, to chase and wrestle with during the day. This little kitty is now a whopping 26 pounds with long fur and claws! No worries, they would chase each other, wrestle and play hide and go seek for the next 9 years, until one day Abby couldn't jump up anymore to do the wrestling part. As I look back, it was the first sign of trouble. I just thought she was getting old and slowing down.

One day, while out for our daily walk, Abby suddenly threw her left leg out to the side like she had a cramp in her muscle or a thorn in her paw. I thought it might be a muscle cramp so I rubbed it, gave her love, and almost instantly we were walking back to the house completely normal, just like nothing had happened. Several days later, it happened again. This time I thought I'd better take her to the Vet to see what's happening…and she was also due for a bath and toenail clip. Just a routine visit in my mind. Not so.

My husband and I had barely walked in the door when the Vet called and asked us to return. Well, we knew this couldn't be good news, but we had no idea how devastating the actual news would be. Our Vet showed us the x-ray of Abby's leg. There was a tumor inside and around the bone of her left leg. It was Osteosarcoma. Cancer. Aggressive and malignant. There was no cure. It was then that she offered to put her down that day-right then and there. I will never forget those words…they still echo in my mind when I reflect on that moment in time. After a stare of utter shock and disbelief…we both said: "NO WAY!" She is "Happy Abby" as everyone called her…wagging her tail, ready to go for a ride in the car. I told her I would let her know when it was time…because Abby would tell me with her eyes…

We sought out a second opinion with a dog cancer hospital and the prognosis was still the same. No cure. You could put her through radiation treatments and it might prolong her life 2–6 months…but there was no cure. OK. Now, let's make her last days as happy and fun as we possibly could. Six months prior to Abby's cancer diagnosis, she was diagnosed with Cushing's disease. It was responsible for her gaining 20 pounds. I kept insisting that Geoff was over feeding her, for her to get so fat—so fast! Well, it wasn't Geoff's fault, it was the Cushing's. We put her on a really strict diet, and along with the meds, she had finally dropped the 20 pounds. Now, the cancer. It didn't really seem fair.

So, let the spoiling begin. If there was one thing Abby always wanted and couldn't have…it was cat food. She LOVED cat food. Why do dogs love cat food? Every dog I have ever loved, loved cat food! I finally had to put the cat's food dish in the upstairs laundry room sink because Abby couldn't reach it there! So, Abby enjoyed her cat food…every day. We were told she would only live about 2 more months, so she might as well eat what she wants. Little did we know that she would stay with us for another 9 months! And you guessed it…she gained back the 20 pounds, but was a very happy eater!

As the tumor grew and grew, we stopped taking her for walks because the vet told us her bone could snap. That was my greatest concern and I wanted to avoid the pain she would have if it did indeed break. We provided her a large wooden plank so she could get into the backseat of the Jaguar without any jumping (she now rode in style; air-conditioning, a bigger "cat" and leather seats)…and she got a daily car ride until the last few days. My husband would just put her in the car, roll down the window and drive her around town and the neighborhood to sniff and see all the wonderful sights.

It was only a few weeks later I saw her fall down in the front yard and I panicked. I thought for sure the bone had snapped…the one thing we didn't want to happen. Well, it didn't break, but it was causing her to limp terribly. It was then, I knew it was time. She never did show me with her eyes…she knew I would see it all too clearly. She was very good at hiding her pain. So, I called the vet and told her it was time. We had prearranged for our vet to come to our home. We didn't want her last moments to be on a cold table in the doctor's office, as it was not her favorite place. We wanted her here with us. The vet said she could come over at noon. I asked her what would be the process once Abby left us for the cremation. She told us since it was a weekend that Abby would stay in a cold storage locker until Monday. That was too much to even begin thinking about…so we opted to keep her comfortable and loved for three more days here at home.

Monday came. It always comes. It has for thousands of years. No amount of wishing it away would change its arrival. We fed her some really great steak for breakfast and gave her much love and hugs and belly rubs. She was so happy, still squeaking those darn toys! Noon arrived, just like Monday and so did the vet. I didn't want to let her in. I couldn't open the door. I froze, with the pain in my heart so heavy that I thought I too would stop breathing. My husband had to open the door. Abby was happy to see her and was squeaking her favorite toy and giving her kisses. Do you know how hard it was for me to get her to lay down on her bed so we could put her to sleep? It was the hardest thing I have EVER done in my entire life. Why wouldn't time stand still just for once? As we said our final good-bye for now…I was holding her and in ten seconds…she was crossing The Rainbow Bridge. No more squeaking of toys, no more barking at the door bell, no more wrestling with the monster cat, no more hide and seek, no more daily walks or belly rubs.

I've finally made peace with my decision in realizing it was the greatest extension of my love for her, to ease her suffering from the painful cancer. Her ashes rest here in our home beside her picture. It took me over a year to be able to move her squeaky toys and her bed…in fact, my husband did it while I was out of the country to help save me the pain. Through all of this, I have learned that in healing our deepest grief—we must let Time…be Time.

The reason a dog has so many friends is that he wags his tail instead of his tongue.

—Anonymous

CHELSEA

Mary H

We had a black lab-chow mix. She was wonderful. Even people who didn't like dogs loved Chelsea. She lived to play Frisbee, and would jump to catch it, rarely missing. We played in front of our house all the time. One day my roommate was out playing Frisbee with Chelsea, when she came running into the house hysterical. Chelsea couldn't move her back legs. She had jumped to catch the Frisbee, let out a yelp, and then came down hard. We took her to the vet, and she was diagnosed as having had a "stroke in her spine". They stated that surgery was an option, but could not guarantee it would help her at all. She did not appear to be in pain, no whimpering, but she could not walk. We used a towel like a sling to get her outside, but after a couple of days, she was unable to pee, so we had to take her to the vet to be catheterized. After 2 days of that, we made the decision. It was time. She did not have the quality of life that she loved so much, and you could almost see her asking "Why?" It was an extremely hard decision, but it was the right one. Quality of life is important, for animals as well as people.

HEARTBROKEN

Keith L

The dogs that I have lost have never been because of old age or the need to put them down. They all died tragically.

The Scamp died of epilepsy.

Toby was poisoned.

Taco was hit by a car.

Snoopy was backed over by my ex-wife.

Yogi drank anti-freeze.

With every little friend I lost, it broke my heart. I told the kids I didn't want another dog for that reason. I was just too heartbroken to bear it again. So what happens? Shane asks us to tend Tyke for a weekend and Tyke is still here six years later.

TOGETHER FOREVER

Pamela G
with Leonbergers Midnight Blue, Sunset Sky and Bella Notte

I had two wonderful English Mastiffs, sisters from the same litter: Piper Cheyenne and Cessna Skylark. They were named after the aircraft because my husband is a pilot. They did everything together their whole lives. Both girls weighed in at about 190 pounds, but Cessna thought she was a lap dog. Piper was the alpha. A year ago January, Piper was diagnosed with osteosarcoma. Because it is such an aggressive form of cancer, we were warned we might only have her for 30 days. That turned out to be the case. Although Piper was a giant breed dog, she was very light on her feet, graceful and agile. She started deteriorating from the initial diagnosis. When people say you can see it in a dog's eyes when it's time for them to go, that's true. For Piper, who had hip dysplasia and a knee that made her start to limp, the bone cancer in her arm made it difficult to walk. We walked with her outside to potty, just to be there to help her. One day, she lost her footing and face planted in the lawn. She was a very proud girl and that was an affront to her dignity. That night, she looked at me and told me it was time for her to go. Our vet is a wonderful and compassionate man. He came to our house to help her cross The Bridge. Piper left this world peacefully, being held and petted by those who loved her.

Unfortunately, when I said earlier that my girls did everything together their whole lives, it was true of the osteosarcoma as well. This March, Cessna was diagnosed with osteosarcoma in the exact same spot on her arm as Piper's, just the other arm. We were devastated. Cessna was the softest, sweetest creature on this earth. She would get upset with me if I got out the fly swatter to kill flies, because I was being mean to the flies. She would hide behind the couch for 10 minutes. Once she was diagnosed, she started to go downhill immediately. It was like, once the word was out, the disease just took over. We were able to keep Cessna with us for 6 weeks after her diagnosis. Again, we knew she would tell us when it was her time. As with Piper, I stayed with her virtually every minute for the last weeks of her life. Cessna was always a klutz. Where Piper was graceful, Cessna was very uncoordinated. There was one day that I walked with her outside to go potty, and I could see that she was afraid that she would fall. That night she gave me the look that said it was time to go. Waiting for the vet to come to the house the next day, we sat talking with Cessna. She was never a licker, and kisses were a rare treat in our house. My husband was having a very hard time letting her go and was questioning whether she had a few more days left. Cessna put her paw on my husband's arm and gave him 30–40 kisses. That was all the confirmation we needed. It was her way of telling him it was okay and thank you. She left with her head cradled in my husband's lap, surrounded by all of our love.

I'm typing this as I'm bawling my eyes out. These girls were my daughters, my friends and my life. My heart breaks every day that they were taken so soon from me. Piper was only 5½, and Cessna died a month before her 7th birthday.

For me, the answer about when is it time to put your dog to sleep is when you're keeping them alive for you, instead of for them. If I had kept them longer, they would have endured pain and sadness. I had to love them enough to let them go, because that was what was best for them. They gave me unconditional love their whole lives, right up to their last breath. I couldn't do less for them.

SUZIE AND SADIE

Doris F

Both of our dogs had to be put to sleep because of various health problems.

We waited too long because we couldn't bear to face the finality of our decision. Because dogs are our faithful friends, no matter what, it is hard to say good-bye. We were selfish in thinking only of ourselves and our feelings. When we finally faced the reality and seriousness of their problems, we realized how much they were suffering. Even as sick as they were, they still showed their love and devotion by trying to be their old self. It was one of the most difficult things we had to do, but we knew they could finally rest in peace. We still remember them and some of the things they used to do; but in the long run, we knew we made the right decision.

We were sad and in mourning for a while, but time has a way of healing the sadness. Our faithful friends, Suzie and Sadie, will always be in our hearts. About three years ago, we rescued Goldie, our Jack Russell, from the animal shelter. She has brought a lot of joy and laughter into our home.

GOOD-BYE, JUNIOR

Brenda H

I recently had to say goodbye to Junior, my adorable miniature pinscher companion of 15 years. Junior was with me in California, and then came back to England with me. He endured 6 months of quarantine in the UK, which I felt so bad about, but that was the law then. Junior went ahead of me via British Airways to England, whilst I sorted out business in California. I went to see the Dog Communicator, who confirmed that Junior knew I hadn't abandoned him and that I would come for him as soon as I was able. To see him again after 6 months was a most wonderful reunion. Tears flow as I type. Junior adapted to life in England, loved the country walks and when the sun shone, he was out there basking in it (he was a California dude). One time he over-did it and almost had a heat stroke! Junior's mind was sound, but his body gave up. His back legs were failing him and he could no longer follow me upstairs as he always did at bedtime, nor could he go on our daily walks without me carrying him.

I didn't mind carrying him and helping him to go outside, but I didn't want him to suffer either. So I took him to the vet who said he had serious neurological problems, and did I want to put him down right at that moment. Of course I didn't—I wasn't prepared for that and I needed time.

I finally decided that it was his time, but to look into his eyes and tell him was so very hard. On Junior's last day, my brother and daughter came to say their good-byes and I couldn't stop crying. I was a coward at the end. I sat in the car with my other miniature pinscher, Minnie, and let my brother be with him. I just didn't want to see him go. I had been there for my last two dogs, and just couldn't go through that again.

The pain will never go away, his memory will always remain and the happy times we shared will never be forgotten. Every dog we have in our lives is special, unique and God's gift to us—DOG=GOD. I hope that sharing this experience will in some way help prepare someone to say goodbye to their dear and trusted friend. It is one of the hardest things we have to do in life. I believe that when my time comes, Junior, Wynston, Sophie & Smudge will be there waiting to greet me.

Minnie now has a new friend, Morgan. He is no way another Junior, but he has his own special personality too.

PRECIOUS

Lizz N

I had a beautiful white Pomeranian that we purchased outside a Wal-Mart in Victorville, CA.

We were looking to purchase a home out there, where it was more affordable. After 6 months of driving out every other weekend from Monrovia to Victorville, we ended up buying not a house, but instead, two of the most wonderful pets that changed our lives forever.

Precious was diagnosed early on with kidney problems. She lived on a special KD dog food diet for 3 years. I was married at the time, and able to afford it. She and Bubbles (the other Victorville dog) had 2 litters of puppies. Needless to say, we kept all the pups and 3 of them survived.

After my divorce, I wasn't able to afford to give her the KD dog food, and she started to not be herself anymore. She was the reason I did not go after what belonged to me in the divorce. My ex-husband said if I went after my stuff, he would fight for custody of Precious and the other dogs in court. I knew he did not care for them as much as I did, so I backed off and got pretty much nothing. Its ok, I got my dogs. Precious would be with me when I cried, and I would talk to her when I had problems. Being a single mom and trying to make it on your own, with no help from anyone, is hard. Precious was by my side each step of the way.

Soon, she was starting to become more lethargic and was very skinny. One thing I did notice is that there was no more color inside her mouth. She still did her motherly duties and took care of all the pups, including my son and me. She would watch me cry, and I would talk to her about my problems. I took her for her routine check-up at the vet and they did the blood work.

They told me that she was not doing well at all, and that it did not seem like she would make it through another month. I told them they had to do something, that there had to be something that could be done. They sent me to an animal hospital in Murrieta, CA where she underwent dialysis and a blood transfusion. $1,500.00 later (that I did not have), she came home and she looked as good as new. She was walking and smiling again, as if nothing was wrong. But the hospital had told me that this would not last, that I would need to contact UC Davis to see about a kidney transplant. I did not care how much it was going to cost; I was ready to take out a loan to pay for this, since by that time I was making good money at a great job.

Precious came home on a Sunday, and I contacted UC Davis on Tuesday morning. Sadly, she took a turn for the worse on Tuesday night and we had to put her down. That evening, I was in school doing an Algebra final when I got numerous calls on my cell phone from my son, and also from my boyfriend at the time. Precious had had a seizure and was back in the hospital. They said that they could do another blood transfusion, and hopefully it would last another 3 days to see if we would be able to get her into UC Davis. However, my son, at the age of 15, made the hardest decision of all and said "Mom, no one is home during the day, and we get home late. If we do another blood transfusion, she may have another seizure while we are not home, and then she will really suffer". He was right. We were being so selfish in trying to keep her alive, because she kept our souls alive. I regret not being there with her when she was laid to rest, because if I would have seen her one more time, I would have made every excuse in the book to not have her put down.

I cried myself to sleep for 4 months straight. It was unhealthy. I have only been able to visit her at the cemetery once, because I can't bear the pain. It has been almost 5 years since this happened and I can't think of her without crying, like I am now.

Your pets will be loyal to you even while on their death bed. But we can't be selfish and let them suffer with pain. They can't speak to us to tell us they are in pain, but even through the pain they are there with us to be the loyal and lovable animals they truly are. When I lost my job, I had to find homes for her hubby and pups. I found great homes for them, but the loss and pain in my soul will never go away. The beauty about loving animals is the joy you get from loving them and them loving you in return. The not-so-beautiful part is the pain of losing them. It is almost as bad as losing a loved one that you know, if not worse. There is a light though—the light that stays in your heart is the beauty of it all. I started to feel better when I rescued a small dog from a busy highway. Even though I had her pups with me, rescuing this other dog helped me put her to rest in my mind and soul. Sometimes, getting a new pet soon after the loss of your pet seems to help with the pain and eases the soul.

Animals share with us the privilege of having a soul.

—Pythagoras

ALLY

Pam L

Unfortunately, we had to go through the experience of putting our dog down earlier this year.

Let me tell you a little about my baby, Ally. Oh my gosh, it was love at first sight. She was a tiny Yorkshire terrier. I had never had pets as a child, so this was really a new and exciting experience for me. We had her home for a few days and noticed she was not playing or eating like little puppies do. Our veterinarian told us she was a "Shunt" puppy, meaning inbred and a puppy mill dog. Harry and I took her to a specialized hospital that performs operations on this type of problem. They cut her open from neck to tail to insert a special piece of metal to correct the severe problem. Her liver was not filtering properly. Now you have to know, Harry and I were told we could put her down or do the operation. No Discussion for ME! I was so in love at that point.

The doctor said she would always have the brain of a 6 week old puppy and probably would not live her full intended life. I did not care…I loved her so much.

From that day forward, I hand fed her twice a day and she made us very happy. We bought a sister to join her and they were inseparable. Sophie was our newest member and loved Ally as much as we did.

Moving along, Ally had her challenges through her 10½ years on this earth with us. But, she always came through, to the amazement of her doctors.

I noticed her not eating and having trouble breathing, to the point of gasping for air at times. I was in denial and made excuses in my mind. You see, she was never going to leave us (in my mind). I decide to take Ally in to have her family vet look her over. I already knew her heart was enlarged, and had her on heart meds. It was 2pm on Tuesday, the 17th of March—St. Paddy's Day—one I won't forget.

Dr. D. looked her over and then looked at me. He said "Pam, its time. She's tired and needs to go home." Just like that! I intended for her to go home with me, with more meds, a miracle medication. I wanted her to have a heart transplant. Do you see the desperation?

She was too weak and tired to even raise her head. I asked the doctor to give me a minute to make a call. I called my daughter and she came to help me with my final good-byes.

I didn't want to call my husband because he was attending a conference, and the last thing he needed was a hysterical wife and the thought of losing our baby.

So, painfully I held her and told her many times over, "Ally, your Daddy and I have loved you from the first moment we laid eyes on you. We will always love you, and now it's time to go and rest without the pain". I held her as the doctor administered the final drug. She went limp in my arms, and it was over. I have to admit that I don't remember a whole lot after, except I could not drive home and the Veterinarian called my husband with concern. Yes, that's how he found out!

I have some comfort today because I know she was suffering. Selfishly, I wanted to take her home that day and pretend it was all a dream. When do you know it's time? As I look back now, she tried to tell me. I probably should have taken her in 2 or 3 months earlier. I DID look into her eyes and I saw. She stopped eating, drinking and "Hey, Big Sign", but I kept feeding her thru a small straw. I knew "when" and I ignored that. Sometimes we have to let go and set them free. She DID tell me.

BABY

Laura M

I recently had to put my dog, Baby, to sleep because she had Cancer. Baby was a mixed Shepherd and 12 years old. We are dog lovers, and Baby came to us by taking her from the neighbor's front porch one night, after they left her out in the rain two times when she was only a few months old. She grew up with our two other Pit bulls: my female Pit bull Dolly, and male Pit bull Spike. They raised her as their own. They never fought and they loved each other very much.

Baby was a little overweight, but she loved to walk and play all the time. She demanded a lot of attention and was very needy. One day, we noticed that she didn't want to eat in the morning, and she left some of her food in the afternoon. That was very unusual for her, because she loved to eat and would always try to steal everyone else's food.

I took her to the Vet, and was present when they did an ultrasound on her stomach. The Vet's first reaction was, "Oh! This is what I didn't want to see!" Her Cancer was so spread out that it was also pushing her spleen to the side. I didn't want to start crying in front of everyone and so I held back my tears and all I could say was, "Well, I know I gave her a good life". Twelve years is more than a 70lb dog would normally live.

I took her home and she was on pain medication. My sister, mother and I talked about it and said that we didn't want to see her suffer. For the next three weeks, there were days that she would eat all her food and sometimes just little. She still wanted to go for walks. The Vet told us that when she didn't want to eat anymore, then that was the day. So, came April 27 and she didn't want to eat anymore. We made the decision to take her in the next day. That morning, she was throwing up bile and it was so hard to see that. So, with all the pain in my heart, I sat with her for awhile and said my good-byes to her. Now we are going thru the same thing with Dolly, my Female Pit bull. She also has Cancer and bad arthritis. We are trying to keep her as comfortable as possible. We watch that she doesn't walk thru the kitchen floor, because her back legs are weak and she slips. But as long as she eats and she wants to go out and walks, even though it's just to the front yard and back, we will hold on to her for as long as we can. Dolly is 14 years old and like I said, we know that they had a good life. Spike is 16 years old right now and he is our baby. When that day comes, it is definitely going to be the hardest day of lives.

One thing is for sure: If you know that you have given your pet all the love and attention that you possibly could, then don't let them suffer. When they can't walk or don't want to eat anymore, it's time to let them go. It's very hard to tell with them, because they can hide the pain so well. My advice to you is to act normal the day you decide it's time, because they can sense the sadness and they will try and pretend to be okay, and then you'll say, "Just One More Day".

MY BEST PAL, SHEP

Jason M

This is something I'm still dealing with, although my last day with Shep was over three and a half years ago.

Shep was my best friend ever for 11 years. I got him as a rescue puppy from two acquaintances that picked him up from the pound, then realized they couldn't keep him. I was a bachelor and a bit of a loner, and he instantly became my constant companion. We went everywhere together. Walks in the morning, and at night. Hikes in the mountains of Squaw Valley. He hung out at the job site when I was painting a house, or at times, he'd just wait for me in the truck.

He also became a friend to all who met him. Shep had so much personality and intelligence that he truly lit up a room. Even as a Shepherd-Doberman mix and over 100 pounds, he was so full of happy energy that small children were naturally drawn to come right up and pet him.

Once he turned 11, Shep was spending more and more hours sleeping and looking lethargic. At other times, he was his normal self, but the lethargy continued until I took him to see the vet. The doctor had 26 years of experience. He gave Shep a quick exam by running his hands around Shep's body and abdomen, and then he told me there was a large growth in his abdomen. I was quite surprised, especially that I hadn't noticed it during my regular petting and hugging sessions with my best pal. Then the doctor added that it was likely a cancerous tumor and perhaps had even spread to other organs, like the heart, lungs, kidney, etc. Shep was slowly dying. He said that he'd do an exploratory, and hopefully remove an isolated cancer, but if it had spread throughout Shep's body, we'd have to talk about decisions. The doctor said, in his experience, once the cancer had spread, most dogs only had a few months to a year of life, and the quality of life was often miserable due to their inability to feel good, to eat normally, to stand and walk, to control their bladders, etc.

I didn't want to think about it, but agreed that the exploratory should be done right away. The next day, Shep was taken into the operating room. Hours later, the doctor called to inform me that the cancer was the size of a grapefruit and had spread everywhere, that even after removing the tumor, Shep had perhaps six months and that it would likely be an awful time. He asked me to consider euthanizing for Shep's sake and gave me his whole-hearted, 26 years worth of seeing these results, recommendation.

I was floored. Two days before, I had no idea this would be a decision I'd be making. The thought of putting my best friend to sleep forever was just as unthinkable as having Shep go through a major surgery only to suffer for the next few months until a slow and painful death awaited him. I couldn't decide, but I had to. In the end, I took the doctor's advice. He administered the lethal dose, and I stood there petting him, crying and mentally asking Shep to go with God and wait for me.

I took his body home, dug a big hole in the backyard and buried my best friend. It's been over three-and-a-half years, and I still question that decision. I feel like I put too much emphasis on the expert opinion. Perhaps Shep would have had two or three more years, and maybe they wouldn't have been so bad. Or perhaps he would've had a few months, and they would've been absolutely awful like the doctor predicted. What a terrible decision to have to make. I feel for anyone who faces this choice. If the clock was turned back, I wonder if I would make the same choice. Something in my heart tells me Shep would have wanted to live with me more. That's the hard part to live with, and I've beaten myself up over it many times.

My only advice, and the thing that makes me feel a little better about it, is this; I know I loved Shep as well as I humanly could in the time we had together. Many other pet owners know this feeling. I also know I made some poor decisions, and perhaps my final decision was one of those. However, I loved him to the extent of my capabilities and I still do. We're always together at some level.

Everyone has to make their own decision here. I don't believe there is any right or wrong choice. They both have benefits, and they both have consequences. I pray that one day, hopefully in many, many years, I'll see Shep again. I believe he'll forgive me as I'm still learning to forgive myself.

SABRINA AND BEAR

Lisa M

Sabrina was a yellow lab we bought from a pet store because my daughter fell in love with her, and I could not resist my daughter's heart when it came to bringing the dog home. She was a loving puppy that learned quickly, but never stopped licking. Even though everyone else said she would stop with age, that never happened. We took her to water but her biggest thrill was diving into our pool, going under water to fetch the sinking socks. She actually held her breath and would swim the length of the pool while on the hunt for whatever items we sent into the water for her to fetch. I was a single parent and Sabrina earned her keep for life at an early age, when she barked and scared off would-be robbers at 1:00 in the morning. She lived with us for 12 years before a lump appeared on her neck. When we took her to the cancer specialist, they said they could do all kinds of operations, but due to her age, they did not think it would make much difference to the extension of her life. We decided the best thing to do was just let her live happy, without painful surgeries that would not make a difference. She stayed with us another 4 months before she went blind. The funny thing about her being blind was she still wanted to play fetch, and as long as she could hear where the ball was, she would bring it back. About 3 months later, she came to me and told me it was time and that this was the day. On the way to the vet, she laid her head across the console onto my lap and stayed there just as sweet and gentle as ever, looking up at me all the way there, as if she was saying goodbye. The vet said that she would not make it through the night so, we let her go.

Bear was a chocolate lab we got a year after Sabrina, from the same pet store. This time, it was because she had gotten too old and too big. No one was adopting her, and they were getting ready to send her to the puppy mills to become a breeder. Bear could hardly walk when we got her home, due to so much time in the cage and no exercise. Sabrina, Bear and my daughter were the best of friends within just a short time. From jumping off the diving board together, to just sleeping together with my daughter, they were buddies. Bear was a funny dog with so much personality, you could not help but want to pet her and love her. After Sabrina passed, I started taking Bear with me everywhere I went, and she loved it! After about 2 months, she stopped eating and I was trying to feed her anything she wanted. But still, she would not eat. I took her to the vet; they looked at her gum line and determined that she had cancer of the spleen. Then a little known fact about spaying a female dog was also part of the problem. The vet we had taken her to as a puppy to get spayed did not remove all of the parts he should have, so she got breast cancer. The X-ray showed that she also had spots on her lungs. They were ready to put her down and I knew she was not quite ready to go. I took her home and tried steak, cat food, cheese, eggs—anything to get her to eat, but she refused and was beginning to stumble when she walked, due to a lack of energy and food. I had the opportunity to take her to the park for 2 days prior to having to put her down. The days were spent enjoying the sun. On the second day, I told a mother who was walking by that it was her last day and if she had some kids that could come by and pet her, it would really make her feel better. She brought about 8 kids back that all started to love and pet Bear. Bear turned to me with such a happy smile on her face, it made me feel better about the last day I got to spend with her. When I took her to the vet, she did not want to go. It was as if she knew it was time but did not want to leave me, nor I her.

The moral of my story is that no matter what the time of the decision is, it is not easy. I think we have more compassion and decision capabilities for our animals than we do for other humans that we love. I am extremely grateful to my animals for loving us unconditionally and for as long as they could. I know when they leave, it opens up space for another animal to receive love, and for us to give it.

BLACKJACK

Karen K

I am writing to you about my Dog, B.J., short for BlackJack . He is the last dog I had before my current love dog, Eli.

B.J. was a Dalmatian, loved by everyone because of the movie "101 Dalmatians", which came to theaters when he was about three or four years old. He was constant motion. He did not sit so you could pet him, but he would back up so you could scratch his butt before he took off. BJ was still constant motion at age 11. He began coughing kind of funny, like something was in his throat, so we went to the vet and he had a cancerous tumor between his throat and heart. Everything else was healthy and normal. He did quite well for 7 months, and then the coughing worsened. He kept trying to clear his throat. Soon, he was not as energetic and then he couldn't jump up on the bed. I knew the cancer was advancing. I lowered the mattresses to the floor, which worked. But the look on his face was so revealing. He seemed to be asking me what was happening. He would still be energetic for walks and especially car rides, his favorite thing in the universe. I started to spoil him with any treat he wanted. Within another week, I could tell at times he was uncomfortable at night. He did not look well for 2 days and he was lethargic and ill at ease. Then the day came when he did not eat. That is when I knew it was time. To me, that is one of the signs, believing that is what an animal would do instinctively when they know time is near. I made that awful decision to go to the Vet. On the car ride (his favorite thing) over to the Vet's office, he came alive like nothing was wrong, though you could see some signs of a weaker dog. This, of course, made it almost impossible to make the final decision to ensure that his last days were not in pain. Almost.

I have never been sure that it was the exact right day, but all the signs at home were of a dog that was failing. What I do know for sure is that there was no prolonged suffering.

When I arrived home from the vet with a broken heart, this note was on my computer. An e-mail from my Mom that she had sent, and at the bottom it said, "Written By BJ". (She had no idea that I had put him down minutes before. This was my sign that all was as it should be.)

If A Dog Were Your Teacher

If a dog were your teacher, these are some of the lessons you might learn:

When loved ones come home, always run to greet them.

Never pass up the opportunity to go for a joyride.

Allow the experience of fresh air and the
wind in your face to be pure ecstasy.

When it's in your best interest, practice obedience.

Let others know when they've invaded your territory.

Take naps and stretch before rising.

Run romp and play daily.

Thrive on attention and let people touch you.

Avoid biting, when a simple growl will do.

On warm days, stop to lie on your back on the grass.

On hot days, drink lots of water and lay under a shady tree.

When you're happy, dance around and wag your entire body.

No matter how often you're scolded, don't buy into the guilt
thing and pout. Run right back and make friends.

Delight in the simple joy of a long walk.

Eat with gusto and enthusiasm. Stop when you have had enough.

Be loyal.

Never pretend to be something you're not.

If what you want lies buried, dig until you find it.

When someone is having a bad day, be silent,
sit close by and nuzzle them gently.

FRANCINE

Pam R

I currently work in a Veterinary Clinic for small animals, so unfortunately I do deal with a lot of loss.

From my own personal experience with losing four-legged babies, I feel that they will let you know when it is time to let go. I had a little Bichon-Maltese cross "Francine". She had pancreatic cancer. We had a wonderful vet at the time. Francine would be so lethargic and he would get her all perked up again. Finally one night, I could tell she was on the downward spiral yet again. I was holding her, and just the way she dropped her head against my chest and looked up at me, I knew that she was telling me that she had had enough. (That was 14 years ago, and I still can recall and feel that look.)

At the clinic, there are of course the obvious cases that come in. But there are also the ones whose owners have to make the difficult decision. Sometimes, there is a chance that their lives could be extended for a bit thru heroic measures, but as a responsible owner—you have to decide if you are extending the critter's life for the critter, or for your own needs. I certainly would not want to exist once my quality of life had deteriorated.

As long as pain meds are keeping your pet comfortable, and she is still eating and drinking, continue to love and enjoy her company.

They never talk about themselves,
but listen to you while you talk about yourself,
and keep up an appearance of being
interested in the conversation.

—Jerome K. Jerome

MISS ELL DEE—THE BEST DOG EVER

Roca W

The best dog ever, LD, was 18½ years old when her kidney failure occurred. Two vets had informed me years before that she would probably die of kidney disease, as her blood tests indicated they didn't work very well. I can say, looking back, I was too selfish and made her live a year longer than she should have. In the end, she was blind and deaf, and puking her guts out every day.

On February 14, Valentine's Day, my husband of 10 years died. I was 32 and widowed. My feet didn't hit the ground for two years after that, when my father was diagnosed with terminal large cell carcinoma. Through it all, LD was my comfort. She was stability.

I drove my father to radiation every Friday and cried all the way home each time. He was the only real parent I had, loving me unconditionally. LD was there to continue loving me unconditionally when my father died.

Two years after that, my mother died following a car crash. I inherited the burden of being the trustee of my eldest brother's finances. He was in a nursing home at the time. Brain damaged from a bicycle accident. He didn't really get that I was his little sister.

About two years after that, my brother died. Again, LD was there. My rock.

Two years later, after LD lost her hearing, I came home to find her on a pillow on the bed. I called to her. Nothing. I jiggled the bed. Nothing. I yelled. Nothing. I touched her to see if she was breathing. She slowly opened her eyes and stretched and wagged her tail.

She began throwing up every day. I took her to the vet. He said, "It's time." I looked at him and told him I understood what he was saying and I agreed in my head, but my heart wasn't ready. Could I have one more day?

He agreed. I went home and sobbed. LD was right there, comforting me, cuddling with me.

The next day, I took her to the vet and put my arms around her on the cold, steel table. He tied her front leg off, got a big syringe and filled it. He shaved her to find a good vein. As the fluid entered her body, it slowly relaxed and then crumpled. She was gone.

While forcing myself to drive to work 3 days later, I felt warmth and laughter and light. There were comforting arms around me. It was LD saying, "I love you" and "Good-bye."

So many years later, I still tear up when I think of her. Miss Ell Dee. The best dog ever.

A dog is the only thing on this earth that loves you more than he loves himself.

—Josh Billings

THANK THEM FOR THEIR LOVE

Denyse O

Sadly, I have had many experiences where I had to make the decision to say good-bye to my beloved animals. When I knew the time was coming, and after doing everything possible and maintaining a decent quality of life for my animal, I sat with my animal and had the "talk". I thanked them for all of the love and memories that would remain with me throughout my lifetime, and I asked them to please let me know when they were ready, that I really needed their help.

What I have learned is our animals have no fear to pass over—it is us having to let them go. Every time that I made that dreadful appointment, my animal would do something that would absolutely validate the decision (in other words silently telling me it was OK and they were ready, and sometimes I even heard a voice).

We will always want to remember our pets in the best way we can, not the memory of them not walking, not eating or not even having the energy to wag their tail!

HENRY

Missy

My Henry was 15 and had several serious health threats over the years; but being a mutt, he was fairly resilient. He was half Schnauzer, half Lhasa Apso and he was pretty cute, if I do say so myself. He had not been feeling well, and one morning, I noticed a lump under his chin (for lack of a better anatomical name). I took him to the regular vet (who, in my estimation, was a little more interested in the money than the animal). He took an X-Ray and said he didn't see anything. Henry had not been eating as well for a couple of days, but he was still pretty perky. The next morning, when I woke and let him outside, he was too weak to stand and go potty. I took his temperature and he had a fever (even for a dog) and I was at the Vet when they opened. Fortunately, the regular vet was off and the other vet in the office, who I really liked, saw him. She looked at his X-Ray from the day before and asked me if I had seen it. As she started to point, I saw the lesions as clear as day. She sent me to a specialist and while we were there, Henry had a seizure. We medicated him and I took him home on antibiotics and seizure meds. He had another pretty big seizure and I took him to the Emergency Vet Clinic. They kept him overnight. About 3:00 am, I woke myself up talking—I was dreaming Henry was having a seizure and I was saying "I'm coming, baby, I'm coming." Silly, huh? I had someone cover for me at work until I could pick him up and take him to the vet's office for the day. As it turned out, he had had a seizure around 2:30 am. He did well until around 5:00 pm, when he had another seizure. That is when I made the decision. I couldn't stand to see him suffer like that.

I brought him home and he seemed good. I took him to the neighbors to say good-bye as he was well loved by them. We woke up in the night and I gave him a burger patty I'd brought home, which made him very happy. He didn't even seem to mind his IV saline lock that he had been sporting for a couple of days. He looked so good that I almost changed my mind. But I knew better.

I kept my appointment. It was a beautiful November day here in Florida—sunny, cool and a nice breeze. We went outside under a tree on a quilt the vet had. We sat there. I held Henry and petted him. Then, when I was ready, the vet gave him the drugs. It was quick, and I'm so glad I was there to hold him. He'd been my "baby" for 15 years, so I couldn't let him do this alone. I grieved for him for what seemed to me to be a long time, but again, he was my little one. I still carry a favorite photo of him in his Christmas antlers.

I guess my point is—you will know when it's time. Keeping your "baby" comfortable and enjoying the time left is the most important thing.

SUNNIE FOR SHORT

Deb E

It is true—dogs will let you know when it's time. It will first be in their behavior, then in their eyes. When they stop enjoying their food, when they want to go lie in their bed alone and not be with you, when they seem tired but cannot sleep—these are tell-tale behaviors. But you will know for sure when they look at you in a particular way. It will be a look in their eyes that asks you to help them make the journey over The Rainbow Bridge...and you will know.

I know these things are true because I experienced them first-hand with Sunshine (Sunnie for short), the sweetest little beagle ever. She was my buddy, a spoiled-rotten, couch-potato princess of a dog. We had 10 wonderful years together, but shortly after her 10th birthday, she developed an almost insatiable thirst for water. It seem as though I was filling her water dish constantly. Our vet did blood tests and diagnosed Sunnie with Cushing's disease. It could be somewhat controlled with medication, but the real problem was that Cushing's in dogs is usually caused by a tumor on the pituitary or adrenal gland. In Sunnie's case, the vet suspected a tumor on the pituitary gland.

It wasn't very long before the disease progressed beyond the medication's ability to control it. All Sunnie wanted to do was drink, and I had to coax her to eat. (This was highly unusual, because she had always been a real chow-hound...she LOVED mealtimes!) To make a long story short, Sunnie was losing interest in her food because she couldn't smell it anymore...the pituitary tumor grew rapidly and blocked her nasal passages.

Then one day I noticed a discharge from her nose. She stopped eating altogether that same day. I took her to the vet's office, because I thought that, on top of the rest of her problems, she had caught a cold. But the latest verdict wasn't nearly that simple. The tumor had invaded her nasal passages and was causing the discharge.

My vet suggested at this time that it might be best to euthanize Sunnie, but I wasn't ready. It's not that I didn't trust the doctor; she is a truly caring and compassionate woman. But something told me it just wasn't time yet. I was sure I could get Sunnie to eat, and besides...it just wasn't time yet!

Over the next few days, however, Sunnie showed me that I was wrong. I was being selfish, I suppose. Sunnie grew weaker, despite my efforts to get her to eat. One evening when I took her outside, she stood there on the lawn and looked at me, then sort of toppled over onto her side. She just lay there, not having the strength to stand up again. And she looked at me...and I knew. With that deep gaze into my eyes, she was asking for my help, and I knew.

The next morning, I called the vet for the last time. Our appointment was for 4 PM that day...a whole day to wait, to second-guess myself, to feel guilty for what I was about to do. I had to carry Sunnie to the car that afternoon because she didn't have the strength to walk. When we arrived at the office, I went to lift her out of the car, but to my amazement she jumped down and walked across the parking lot on her own. But in the waiting room, she couldn't get up onto the settee, so I sat on the floor with her. She managed to wriggle onto my lap, and I held her while we waited. I spoke softly to her as I petted and cuddled her. I told her what a good girl she had been her whole life. I told her she was about to meet Jesus, and that she was to tell Him all about how she loved to chase rabbits and bark at joggers on the road and grab dirty socks from the laundry basket. Most of all, I told her over and over again that I loved her.

The waiting room was full that day, and we waited a long time. I guess I made people cry. I guess I was crying, too...a man offered me his handkerchief. Finally, it was our turn. I was prepared to carry Sunnie into the exam room, but she walked one last time. The doctor instructed the vet tech to hold Sunnie, and she told me I shouldn't stay. But I needed to stay. Holding my Sunnie as she passed from this life was the final thing I could do for her. Freeing Sunnie from the body that had betrayed her was the final gift I could give her.

This was the hardest thing I have ever done. I left the vet's office with only Sunnie's collar and leash. I still have them. I have another dog now, and she's wonderful in her own way. But she will never replace Sunnie in my home or in my heart.

Every dog's story is unique, but I do know that your pet will tell you when it's time. Just listen with your heart.

OUR TWO LABS

Peggy S—*Mommy* to:
Precious, Ebony, Smokey, Sammy and Hazel—all at The Rainbow Bridge,
and Java, Pickles and Tuffy who are now making my life bearable and
giving me someone to cuddle and love.

I have personally had to help 2 of my Labs to The Rainbow Bridge. The first one (Precious) was just getting old (she was 16) and I could see her grow weaker with each day. She started having accidents and the look on her face when that would happen was just so sad. She seemed to be ashamed and embarrassed, but of course, I never scolded her. Then she got to the point where she could no longer stand on her own. She would try to get up to take care of her personal business; then she would just fall over in it. She started to not eat or drink and it is true about the look in their eyes. She just seemed so sad and so tired; so I knew that it was time to help her say goodbye.

Then there was our 2nd Lab (Ebony), who developed diabetes. She had to have insulin shots twice a day, but she did well for over a year. She was 10 when we had to help her to The Bridge. She also became weak and started having seizures. She could barely get up and down on her own, and also would not eat or drink. Her eyes told me that she was scared, but also that she was so tired and ready to go. The vet agreed that it was time. She had helped me through a very difficult time in my life when I was going through chemo and I thought that it would kill me to let her go. I sat on the floor at the vet's office and held her head and talked to her while she received the injection. She drew one last deep breath and quietly passed on and I thought that I would die right along with her. But I knew that I did what was best for her. It took me 3½ years before I could let another dog into my life.

I am confident that you will know when your dog wants to be released from this life and move on. It is truly one of the hardest decisions that one has to make for the animals that we love. I still get tears in my eyes whenever I think of any of my beloved pets, but I know that I did my best to give them good lives and to make their final days as comfortable as possible.

I now have another Lab who is 2 years old and 2 other cats and I love them just as much as I did my other pets, but it is still different. They each have a special place in my heart and always will. They all have their own personalities and they certainly all have a way of making themselves special and so loved.

It is our duty to care for our beloved pets right to the end and to help them cross over if need be. It is never easy for us to stay behind and to have to see them go on ahead of us, but it is what we need to do so that they do not suffer. As long as your pet is happy and can wag its tail, she is probably not ready to go. It is when they become weak, tired, and can no longer respond to their loved ones that you will know that they are looking to the other side. I think that one of the hardest things is when they no longer want to eat or drink and even by trying to force feed them, they still refuse. That is definitely a sign that the time is drawing near.

SPIKE

Ramona H.

It was a difficult decision to make, but we knew it was time for Spike to go after he collapsed in my lap. It was heart-breaking, but there was nothing else we could do for him. When he fell in my lap on the couch, he stretched out his legs then cried out briefly. I thought he was having a seizure. When I explained this to our holistic vet a few days later, she said he probably had a mild heart attack. He tried to regain control, and did sit up a little. I called the specialists in Mandeville. I was told to take him to our regular vet to be put on oxygen. I called my son who immediately came over. Spike recognized him and gave him his regular welcome barks. By then, Spike was panting heavily, drooling, and his tongue was a purplish color. It makes me cry all over thinking about this, because the mass was robbing my sweet boy of oxygen. He would have suffocated to death here at home and I couldn't bear to see him suffer that way. I only wish things would have been different, that a miracle would have happened to keep that mass under control. The X-rays showed it had grown three times in size since his diagnosis in August. He only had about two fingers of space for breathing.

When we arrived at the vet, she said there was nothing that could be done for him. We briefly talked about what was happening, and I agreed to let her give him the shot. My son and I were in the room with Spike. I kept petting his head and told him I loved him over and over. The vet said, "He knows you do", and she hugged me twice. I tried not to cry too much before he left us, but it was hard not to. At least he was home with us instead of at the hospital so many miles from home. I never would have forgiven myself had it happened while he was there.

I'd give anything to have Spike (and Sheba) back with me right now. It's been a sad day for me today because we had so much fun last year during the Halloween holiday. It's going to be even harder at Christmas. Our babies bring us so much joy and happiness to our homes, but it's so painful and sad when they're gone.

Our holistic vet told me we would know when it's time for Spike to go because he would have that look in his eyes. I'm not sure if he gave me the look or not, as I didn't have time to think about that. I only know he was struggling to breathe and he looked like he was in a panic, as if pleading for me to help him breathe. Making the decision was one of the hardest things I've ever done. I've always said I could never do that, but when I saw Spike suffering and knowing he'd suffocate, I did what's best for him; not for what I wanted.

KATIE

Shelley T

I am a recently retired flight attendant, and I have been a pet sitter for the last four years. I am proud to say I am taking care of four-legged babies full time now.

Facing the need to put your pet down is one of the hardest things you may ever have to do. I have had a dog my whole life, with the exception of a few years in between when I left home, work, school, etc. Unfortunately, I have lost several in my lifetime. Deciding when is the "right time" is a very difficult thing to do.

I had an old girl, Katie, a Dachshund-Chihuahua mix, she was 17. I rescued her from a girl that couldn't keep her anymore, when she was about 8 months old. I loved that old girl, and she loved me more than life I think. She followed me everywhere. She had a heart murmur for about the last 6 years of her life, and had become nearly deaf, and almost blind, we think. She had a bad cough—the vet told me this was because of the heart murmur, but there was not a lot we could do about it (I have discovered since then that I could have had her on some meds that may have helped). Now that I am so involved with dogs, I am learning a lot of things to ask questions about, that I may have been really ignorant about before. (I so hope you have a good vet that you really like and trust). Katie was plugging along, doing pretty well, but her cough was getting worse, and her eyesight was a little worse. One day, as she was coming into the house, she tripped on a small step that she used to hop over every day of her life. She fell on her poor little face and was bleeding. I could not bear the thought of something like that happening when I was flying and nobody was there for her. One day not long after that, she had a really bad coughing spell, and had a hard time catching her breath.

She was wheezing so much, I just couldn't stand it anymore. That was the time for us—and she is buried in my back yard under a pecan tree.

I sincerely hope my story will help someone. We have lost so many pets that we care for, in just a few years– sometimes it seems like they aren't with us nearly as long as we would love for them to be here. And it is almost as hard for us as the pet sitters of the ones we care for on a somewhat regular basis, because we grow so close to them.

Our task must be to free ourselves—
by widening the circle of compassion
to embrace all living creatures and
the whole of nature and its beauty.

—*Albert Einstein*

AND THEN SHE WENT TO SLEEP

Marcia K

The only downside to falling in love with an animal is when they die. With few exceptions, unless you adopt as a senior citizen, this day will usually come.

My husband died early in life and I do volunteer hospice work with children, typically cancer patients. So when our Border collie, Midnight's Crystal, was diagnosed with an aggressive cancer, at age eleven, I was sure it would be easy for me to know how to handle it and be "O.K." with her impending death.

There's a huge difference between someone dying, and deciding when they die. I couldn't have been more wrong. Somewhere between her high pain threshold, undying love for us, wanting to please us at all cost, and of course, lots of pain medication, it was hard to know "when" it would be time. From hospice experience, the one thing I have never lost sight of is my awareness of how painful cancer really is in the end. I knew I couldn't be selfish in my decisions for her.

Our new puppy, whom I'd put a deposit on in October, was a much planned Christmas present for my son, Anton. On Christmas morning, he got everything one could want or need for a new puppy, except the puppy. Instead, he got a certificate from Santa for a new puppy, along with a letter that explained the puppy was too little to leave its mommy. He also got a phone number and address where "Santa's Puppy Keeper" Sandra lived. Sandra, the breeder, happened to be a first grade school teacher, and was wonderful with my son. Of course, on Christmas morning, Anton immediately had to call to see when he could come and get his new puppy. When he found out it wasn't even born yet, the kid cried all day!

Sandra called on New Year's Eve, while we were on vacation in Wisconsin. The puppies were being born. As soon as we returned from our trip, we drove out to the breeder's ranch with my 7 year-old son in tow, and picked her from the litter at the tiny age of 3 days old. My son named her Crystal, because she was precious like a jewel. The breeder added "Midnight's" to Crystal, so it would look good on paper.

Then began the weekly Saturday treks from home in Newport Beach, CA to Phelan, CA, about 70 miles away, with a video camera in hand. It was about as close to going through a planned pregnancy as you'd want! We brought her home a bit sooner than the breeder wanted, on Valentine's Day. She was just adorable and, true to Border Collie style, usually smarter than the whole bunch of us put together! She was actually on my son's after-school soccer team for a couple of years, and kids would fight over whose side she was on, because she was so good at it!

Crystal's cancer, like Abby's, started in her leg, and twice over the course of several years we had tumors removed, starting when she was about five years old. The second removal and biopsy revealed two types of cancer, but both were slow growing types, so we just went on with life. One day, I noticed what I thought it was an abscessed tooth, but the Vet knew immediately it was cancer again. He said it would be a matter of only a few weeks until it would grow so big that she wouldn't be able to eat. On that day, I promised myself that as soon as I had to start feeding her by hand, then it would be time to let her die with dignity. It sounded easy and rational...

My vision was to let her die at home, in her safe world, but I didn't like the idea of the vet coming out and giving her a shot. It seemed so fast, so unnatural and impersonal. I thought I could obtain something to give her at home, so we could just be together and she'd go to sleep in time, but never wake up. I talked to her Vet, to my brother, who is a Paramedic, and even to our family Doctor, as to what would be the best drug to accomplish this vision. I could see having her burial site already taken care of, in our back yard under the big tree. I would just lay in bed with her, have a glass (maybe a bottle) of wine and we would take our time. By all my various sources, that plan was highly discouraged, because there would most likely be seizures and other side effects that would not make it a peaceful, loving good-bye.

One evening, as I was making one last stop before getting home from work, one of the kids called and said Crystal couldn't use her back legs. I told them to give her a pain pill and I'd be there in 20 minutes. When I got home, she jumped up and came to greet me like nothing was wrong! We went for a walk that night, and though she couldn't go for as long a walk as my other dog, Joey, she seemed just fine. But that night I had to hand feed her.

I worked from home the next day to keep an eye on her. We played ball, even though she couldn't really catch it anymore and her attempts made the tumor bleed. We went for a morning walk, and again I fed her by hand and struggled with the promise I'd made regarding this feeding issue being "the time". She seemed happy and the pain pills were working.

That afternoon I made a quick trip to the store and when I came home, her back legs weren't working again. I called the vet and made "the appointment".

I took her to the beach and we sat for a couple of hours, just spending time together. Finally, we made our way to the Vet's office, toward the end of the day as the sun was setting. Our other dog, Joey, and my son Anton were with us. We took a blanket from my bed that would have all our smells on it, and the Vet had a large cushioned mat on the floor that we put the blanket over. The four of us spent about a half hour just being together, and then we told the Doctor we were ready. He had already shaved a little patch of fur from her back leg and came in with the syringe in hand. I told her I was sorry that I had to do this and hoped it was the right thing.

I swear she gave me a look as if to say, "It's about time you figured this one out"—a grateful, thankful look.

And then she went to sleep.

Quality
of Life

She had no particular breed in mind,
no unusual requirements.
Except the special sense of
mutual recognition that
tells dog and human they have
both come to the right place.

—Lloyd Alexander

QUALITY OF LIFE

Quality of Life means many different things to different people. The term is used to evaluate general well-being and being able to carry out every day activities, despite health problems. Most people agree that it refers to an ability to enjoy life.

Ask yourself what it means to you.

For us, it meant very simply that Abby was spared any further pain. Her cancer was growing, the tumor was spreading rapidly. She didn't moan or bark, or do any of the things that humans can do to convey that they are in pain. All she did was lay there quietly on her doggie bed, licking her paw— constantly licking. That was her way of dealing with her pain. Up until the last few minutes of her life, she was wagging her tail, squeaking her favorite toy, and I'm sure she would have tried to run after a ball if I had thrown it. She still wanted to interact with us.

But it was just a matter of time before her front leg would be so weakened by the tumor that it would snap and break. Just a few days before, she had crumbled to the floor, because her front paw couldn't take the weight. Dawn knew that the time was now. I just wanted one more day—the same as every day.

So, this is where we drew the line on Quality of Life.

Dr. Alice Villalobos has come up with a "Quality of Life' scale, where you can grade your pet from 1 to 10 for seven different categories (10 is the best and 1 is the worst). If your pet has a total score over 35 for the day, that indicates a generally acceptable quality of life. A score below 35 is considered unacceptable. Her article is reprinted here, together with a chart I have designed for you to use. You can download a printable copy of this scale from my web site:

www.justonemoredaythebook.com

*They too are created by the same
loving hand of God which created us.
It is our duty to Protect Them
and to promote their well-being.*

—Pope John Paul II

QUALITY OF LIFE SCALE

By Alice Villalobos, DVM

There is a real need for assessing various levels of quality of life for aging, ailing and terminally ill pets.

Most geriatric animals have one or more abnormal conditions that appear in their senior years and these conditions generally worsen with time. One third of senior pets are obese. Additionally, half of our nation's companion animals over the age of 10 become burdened with cancer and its related treatment issues.

Veterinarians are frequently asked, "When is the right time to euthanize my beloved pet? How will I know?"

A Quality of Life scale may help everyone, especially those in denial, to look at difficult-to-face issues. Caretakers can use this itemized scale to ask themselves if they are able to provide enough help to maintain an ailing pet in a humane way.

Every animal has certain needs that should be recognized and respected.

If we can meet these basic needs at a satisfactory level for our ailing companion animals, then we are justified in preserving the life of the ill pet during its decline.

The goal in setting up the Quality of Life Scale is to provide a guideline so that pet owners can maintain a rewarding relationship that nurtures the human-animal bond.

This scale alleviates owners' feelings of guilt and engenders the support of the veterinary team to actively help in the care and decision making for end-of-life, or "pawspice," patients.

It is up to the veterinary profession and to the pet's caretaker to design an end-of-life pet hospice program that encounters each factor and deals with it openly and honestly. We can use a quality of life scale from one to 10. Ten is the best.

This list, called "HHHHHMM," stands for: Hurt, Hunger, Hydration, Hygiene, Happiness, Mobility, and More good days than bad days. A score above five on most of these issues is acceptable in maintaining an end-of-life program. Each pet's situation needs an individual, kind and supportive approach.

The HMMM Quality of Life Scale (where 1 is the worst and 10 is the best)

Hurt: 1–10

No Hurt: Adequate pain control is first and foremost on the scale. This includes the pet's ability to breathe properly. Most people do not realize that not being able to breathe is ranked at the top of the pain scale.

Some families are willing to provide oxygen therapy at home for their ailing pets and the veterinarian can prescribe it through a medical supply house. Pain control may include oral, transdermal and injectable medications.

Hunger: 1–10

No Hunger: If a pet is not receiving adequate nutrition willingly, by hand or force feeding, then consider placing a feeding tube, especially for cats.

Malnutrition develops quickly in sick animals when the caretaker is not educated. Instruct owners to use blended or liquid diets to help their best friend maintain proper nutritional and caloric intake.

Hydration: 1–10

No Hydration problems: Subcutaneous fluids are a wonderful way to supplement the fluid intake of ailing pets. It may take a few sessions for a pet owner to get the hang of this helpful procedure.

Hygiene: 1–10

Can the pet be kept brushed and cleaned? Is the coat matted? Is the pet situated properly so that it won't have to lie in its own waste after eliminations? Pets, especially cats with oral cancer, can't keep themselves clean, so they get demoralized quickly.

The odor associated with necrotic oral tumors can be offensive and cause social rejection by family members. Antibiotics help reduce foul-smelling infections and using a sponge dampened with a very dilute solution of lemon juice and hydrogen peroxide (to mimic the gentle stroking action of a "mother tongue" on the face, paws and legs) helps soothe and clean cats' fur. Dogs love this type of grooming, too.

Happiness: 1–10

Is the pet able to experience any joy or mental stimulation? It is easy to see that our pets communicate with their eyes. They know what is going on.

Is the ailing pet willing to interact with the family and be responsive to things going on around him? Is the aging cat able to purr and enjoy being on the bed or in one's lap? Is there a response to a bit of catnip? Can the cat bat at toys or look at and follow a laser light?

Can the ailing pet enjoy the upbeat greetings and petting of loving family members? Can the pet's bed be moved close to the family's activities and not left in an isolated or neglected area? Is the pet depressed, lonely, anxious, bored or afraid?

Mobility: 1–10

Ask if the pet is able to move around on its own, or with help, in order to satisfy its desires. Does the pet feel like going out for a walk? Is the pet showing central nervous system problems, seizures or stumbling?

Can the pet be taken outdoors or helped into the litter box to eliminate with assistance? Will a harness, sling or a cart be helpful? Is medication helping?

The answer to the mobility question has variable scenarios. I have met some utilitarian pet owners who are too rigid in the mobility area.

For instance, they regretfully but willingly sacrifice their pet's life rather than elect amputation of a limb. Some pet owners have the honest yet teleological feeling that amputation is mutilation and not fair to the pet. Instead, they allow the pet to bear a painful limb for months before euthanasia.

Then there are cases like Krash, a 12-year-old, male, 90-pound, golden retriever, in Orange County, Calif.

Krash's mobility was already borderline when he entered our pawspice program with osteosarcoma of his left distal radius. His history precluded amputation because of severe degenerative joint disease, degenerative myelitis, (some dogs have had previous bilateral knee surgery) and hip dysplasia. Krash wears a splint to offset a pathological fracture.

The mobility scale can be variable from 1 to 10. The need for mobility seems dependent on the species and breed. Cats and small lap dogs can and do enjoy life with much less mobility than large and giant-breed dogs.

If the pet is compromised and is only able to lie in bed, is there a schedule to change the position of the pet and rotate the body as often as every two hours? Atelectasis and decubital ulcers must be avoided. The nursing care of large immobile dogs is very demanding. Is the bedding material soft enough? Can an egg crate mattress be used and set up properly to avoid decubital ulcers? Is there a role for a pet mobility cart or an Evans standing cart?

These items really make a difference in the quality of life for the pet that has limited mobility yet is alert and responsive.

More Good Days Than Bad: 1–10

When there are too many bad days in a row or if the pet seems to be "turned off" to life, quality of life is compromised.

Bad days are filled with undesirable experiences such as vomiting, nausea, diarrhea, frustration, seizures, etc. Bad days could be from profound weakness caused by anemia or from the discomfort caused by an obstruction or a large, inoperable tumor in the abdomen.

This was the situation with my own dear Australian shepherd, Alfie, who had a huge undifferentiated mass rapidly overtake his liver.

If the two-way exchange needed to communicate and maintain a healthy human-animal bond is just not there, the pet owner must be gently told that the end may be near.

It is very difficult for families to make the final decision to end a beloved pet's life with euthanasia. This is usually avoided when euthanasia is against the pet owner's religious beliefs.

A decision to euthanize can be made clearer to clients if the standard scale for quality of life is set ahead of time and re-evaluated every couple of weeks or every few days as required.

If the pet is slowly passing on with a peaceful tranquility, it may be a satisfactory situation. People often want their pet to pass on naturally at home in their arms or in their own bed. That is OK as long as the pet is just weakening steadily and not suffering to death.

Home euthanasia with a kindly house call veterinarian may be elected.

Hopefully, the concept of a scale for quality of life and our professional guidance can help relieve the angst and regret about a beloved pet's death.

Alice Villalobos, DVM, owns Animal Oncology Consultation Service in Woodland Hills, Calif. She received the 1999 Bustad Companion Animal Veterinarian Award and is associated with VCA Clarmar and Coast Animal Hospitals in Torrance and Hermosa Beach, Calif.

This article first appeared in the September 2004 issue of Veterinary Practice News.

QUALITY OF LIFE SCALE 1–10
(10 = best; 1 = worst)

For Each Day, Put a number in each square, and add up the total. Over 35 = acceptable Quality of Life

	HURT Pain control, breathing	HUNGER Can your pet feed themselves easily?	HYDRATION Is your pet getting enough water? How do they get it?	HYGIENE Is your pet brushed and clean? Is their coat matted?	HAPPINESS Pets communicate with their eyes. Does your pet interact?	MOBILITY Is your pet able to walk around easily?	OVERALL More good than bad	TOTAL For the day
SUNDAY								
MONDAY								
TUESDAY								
WEDNESDAY								
THURSDAY								
FRIDAY								
SATURDAY								

She is your friend, your partner,
your defender, your dog.
You are her life, her love, her leader.
She will be yours, faithful and true,
to the last beat of her heart.
You owe it to her to be
worthy of such devotion.

—Unknown

DEFINING "QUALITY OF LIFE"

by Moira Anderson Allen, M.Ed.

Whenever one considers the painful choice of euthanasia, one is always advised to take the pet's "quality of life" into account. But what is "quality of life"? How can you determine whether a pet is still experiencing a good quality of life—or whether its level of suffering is no longer acceptable? That decision is individual to every pet, and every owner. Following, however, are some factors to consider when attempting to assess a pet's quality of life:

Mobility

An older pet often loses mobility. A dog may no longer be able to climb stairs or hop into a car; a cat may lose the ability to jump onto a bed or chair. At this stage, however, your pet may still be healthy and happy, and you can easily make accommodations for its reduced ability.

If, however, your pet can barely move, that's another matter. Can your pet get to its feet without assistance? Can it sit or lie down without collapsing? Can it walk? Can it handle basic functions, such as squatting on a litter box? Does it whimper or growl if you attempt to move it? I've seen dogs so crippled with hip dysplasia that they literally had to drag their immobilized hindquarters across the floor; this hardly represents the "quality of life" I want for my pets.

Appetite/Eating Ability

Is your pet able to eat? Can it consume enough food (or digest that food) to remain properly nourished? Does it regurgitate immediately after eating? Is it unable to chew, or does it have difficulty swallowing? Does it enjoy eating, or do you have to coax every bite past its lips? A pet that is unable to eat or gain sufficient nourishment from its food is on a slow road to starvation.

Breathing

A number of illnesses, including cancer, can affect the lungs. When a condition causes the lungs to fill with fluid or foreign matter (such as cancer cells), a pet quickly loses its ability to breathe easily or comfortably. You'll notice that your pet may seem to be panting, or that it is laboring to breathe; often, you'll see its stomach or flanks "pumping" as it can no longer breathe with just the chest muscles. It may also experience wheezing attacks. If such symptoms occur, ask for a chest x-ray to determine the condition of the lungs. If the problem is due to an allergy, infection, or asthma, medication may help; if it is due to fluids that are the result of cancer or a heart condition, however, little can be done.

Discomfort

It can be difficult to determine whether a pet is in pain, as animals instinctively mask discomfort as much as possible. You can pick up clues, however, by watching its posture and expression. Does your pet's face appear furrowed or "worried", rather than relaxed and happy? Does it sit hunched or "hunkered" and tense, rather than relaxing and lying down? Lack of mobility can also be a sign of pain.

Another indication of pain is "denning." An animal in pain will seek a safe place (den) where it won't be disturbed by other animals. If your pet has forsaken its usual territories or sleeping places for the back of the closet or a spot under the bed, this may be a sign that it is in pain or distress and feels vulnerable.

A more obvious indication of pain is a pet's reaction to touch. If your pet responds to touch by flinching away, hissing, snarling, or even snapping, this is a clear indication of pain. Sometimes this can indicate a localized pain; if the pet doesn't want to be touched at all, however, it may indicate a broader discomfort.

Incontinence

Many pet owners feel terribly guilty over the natural annoyance they feel when a pet becomes incontinent. They feel they should be more loving, more patient. Incontinence, however, can also be stressful for the pet. As a basic survival mechanism, animals learn not to "mess where they sleep" (for the smell would draw attention to the location of one's den). When an animal can no longer control when or where it urinates or defecates, you can be sure it is not happy with the situation.

Mental Capacity

Older pets occasionally develop signs of diminished mental capacity. They may seem to "forget" things, such as where a toy is located or what a command means. Such a pet may become confused by its surroundings, and this confusion can develop into fear. (In some cases, this "confusion" may be the result of hearing or vision loss, to which both you AND your pet can often adapt.)

Happiness

Determining whether your pet is "enjoying" life is certainly a subjective decision. However, if you have been a keen observer of your pet's behavior and attitude during its lifetime, you are likely to be able to determine when it no longer seems "happy." You'll know when it no longer seems to take any pleasure from its food, its toys, its surroundings—and most of all, from contact with you and the rest of its family. Most pets are tremendously easy to please; when it no longer becomes possibly to raise a purr or a tail-wag, you can be fairly certain that your pet is receiving little joy from life.

Response to Treatment

When a pet becomes ill, our natural response is to provide whatever treatment we can. This may mean tests, medications, even surgery. But drugs have side effects, repeated trips to the vet cause emotional distress, and more invasive treatments take a physical toll. Eventually, we may conclude that our efforts to treat a pet's illness are more stressful to the pet than the condition itself—and that our efforts to save a pet's life are actually diminishing, rather than enhancing, the quality of that life.

Making a Decision

Assessing a pet's quality of life is an ongoing process, not a one-time decision. Initially, we're likely to attempt to compensate for the problems we see. Pain medication may relieve a pet's discomfort and improve its mobility. A change in diet may improve a pet's appetite or provide better nutrition. We may resolve that we're willing to clean up after a pet and carry it wherever it needs to go, for as long as necessary. But eventually such measures will cease to be effective. The process of assessing "quality of life" is really a question of determining (and deciding) when that point has been reached—and what you intend to do next.

It is often tempting, at this point, to postpone a decision still longer by deciding to "let nature take its course." Before choosing that course of action (or inaction), however, it's important to understand that, as a pet owner, you have been thwarting the "course of nature" from the beginning. By ensuring that your pet has food and shelter and is protected from predators, you have already guaranteed that nature will not take its course. By providing medical treatment, you have prolonged the life of your pet far beyond what it could have expected if left to "nature." In nature, an animal that becomes too ill to obtain food or protect itself will perish quickly, though not necessarily comfortably.

Nor does nature necessarily offer an "easy" death even if you choose to let it "take its course" in the comfort of your home. An animal that cannot breathe easily, cannot eat or digest food properly, cannot control its bodily functions, and can scarcely move or enjoy human contact because of pain, is hardly dying "comfortably."

This is really what the "quality of life" issue is all about. By usurping nature's role throughout the life of our pets, we must sometimes also accept its role in determining (and bringing about) the death of a pet. To accept this, we may also have to accept that, in some cases, the quality of life we're really trying to protect is our own: That we're allowing our pet to suffer out of a desire to avoid the anguish we know that we will experience when it dies. And that, ultimately, is the most unselfish act of love we can offer: To end a pet's suffering, we must choose to accept our own.

TIME AND THE JOYS OF LIFE IN DOG CANCER

By Demian Dressler

We are very busy in modern life. It seems as time goes on, the faster it speeds by.

Dog cancer is connected in many ways to time. There is the question that is most pressing: "How much more time do I have?" This is an important piece of information to get, along with the odds of actually gaining this time from a treatment (not all dogs may respond), the odds of side effects, how a treatment will affect your dog's life quality, cost, how often the treatments are, and so on.

Data collection is the first part in thoroughly evaluating a treatment, whether for dog cancer or otherwise.

But not all strategies in the Full Spectrum Approach used in the Dog Cancer Survival Guide are about attacking cancer cells directly. The result of these strategies is life extension

We have another area to consider. This is life quality. Life quality is a critical part of your dog's care. Nobody wants to have a longer life if the life gained is a bad one.

In the Guide we look at many ways to increase life quality after a dog cancer diagnosis. We need to always remember our loved dog's Joys of Life. Here are some of them:

Joys of Life

The joy of eating and drinking. Having hunger satiated and thirst quenched are delightful and are joys. Cancer cachexia (weight loss due to cancer) and dehydration are negatives.

The joy of social relationships with humans and other animals. The love and bonding experiences are joyful for your dog. Depression, loneliness, and the loss of these social interactions are negatives.

The joy of athletic stimulation and movement. Most dogs enjoy the use of their body and physical movement. Not all are athletes, but all enjoy choosing a destination and getting there. Many like walks and play, enjoying the stimulation these provide. Immobility and a lack of desire or ability to move are negatives.

They joy of having normal bodily functions. The ability of the body to do what it is supposed to do is a joy in life. Try taking away your ability to urinate if you don't believe me. The discomfort is excruciating. How about removing the ability to obtain oxygen? Breathing is a joy in life. When normal biological functions are lost, life quality goes down.

The joy of having a healthy mental state. Pain, having unmet needs, dementia, distress, depression, compulsivity, fatigue, and other unpleasant mental states take away this joy. Having a mental state that is normal is a joy in life that is underrated.

The joy of play. This contributes to a healthy mental state. In published research, laughter literally fights disease.

So we need to make sure that we are building activities in our schedule that increase life quality. Another way of saying this is that we need to deliberately increase the Joys of Life for our dogs.

Suppose you have weekly oncologist appointments for chemo for your dog. You have blocked off time twice daily for medication, Apocaps, immune supporting supplements, dog cancer diet preparation, and so on.

When have you scheduled a Joys of Life appointment for your dog? When is this in your Google calendar or your daily planner? What time is allocated and especially reserved for this important appointment?

Dr. Demian Dressler, DVM, owns the South Shore Veterinary Care clinic in Kihei, Hawaii. He is the author of "the Dog Cancer survival guide".

3

Euthanasia
the Final
and
Farewell

EUTHANASIA

When I hear the word euthanasia, I immediately think of Emily Litella, the Gilda Radner character who was hard of hearing, and she would be saying, "Well, what all this fuss about the kids in China?" (Youth in Asia!). I'm trying to find something funny, so I won't cry.

Then, I think of the trial of Dr. Kevorkian who spent eight years in prison for believing a terminal patient had the right to physician-assisted suicide and how we were so divided as a nation in support and opposition. Now, Oregon, Montana and Washington are States that have legalized doctor-assisted suicide. It is such a tough subject even to talk about, never mind act upon.

We're brought up to know that life is sacred, to be cherished. We take care of our elders and do our best to prolong their life with all sorts of new techniques and medications. Causing a human life to end is wrong.

And yet, we must balance that with an understanding that the greatest extension of our love for our pets that we have dominion over is to ease their suffering. Our pets are in our care. We have control of all aspects of their life, and that includes control over their pain and suffering. There is no book, no set of rules that can tell you emphatically when it is time. It's never black or white; there are always shades of grey in making the agonizing decision. And even beyond questions about our pet's health, the amount of pain they are enduring, the amount of care it requires to look after our pet's, there is the ever-present question of money. Can we afford the treatment necessary to bring our pets back to good health, or to stabilize their condition?

I was surprised to learn that a survey by a large pet insurance company showed that accidents accounted for about 5% of dog's deaths; natural death took another 8%, and illness was the cause of death in an additional 35%. What surprised me was that, for 52% of dogs, euthanasia was the cause of death. We never want to part with our pets. But there comes a time when that is the kindest, the best thing we can do for them. It is the greatest expression of our love—to ease their suffering.

So many people told us that pets communicate with their eyes and we would look into Abby's eyes and see when it was time to call the Vet. We never did see that. And so many people have told us that they spent days and weeks, even months, reasoning out in their heads good arguments for keeping their pets "Just One More Day".

There is so much guilt attached to making this decision-guilt that the Vet was called too soon; guilt that the Vet was called too late. All I can say is— Listen To Your Heart.

Here are a few articles that have helped me. My wish is they may also help you.

Love knows not its own depth
until the hour of separation.

—*Kalil Gibran*

EUTHANASIA: THE MOST PAINFUL DECISION

by Moira Anderson Allen, M.Ed.

Many think of bereavement as beginning after loss. For many, however, grief can begin much earlier. Often, it begins the day you realize that your pet is approaching the end of its life—even though the final loss of that pet may still be many months distant.

This stage of grief is especially difficult, because it is without closure. You can't make an effort to "get over it" or "feel better," because the loss itself has not occurred. Thus, no matter how bad you feel, you know that things are just going to get worse. It can be difficult to find comfort during this stage, for even people who understand the pain of bereavement may wonder why you are grieving before your pet has actually died.

Grief for impending loss is complicated by the need to make difficult, painful decisions. How much treatment should you pursue? At what point will treatment cause more trauma than relief? Can you provide the care needed to keep your pet comfortable—and will your pet reach a point where no amount of care can do this? At what point, if any, should you consider euthanasia?

Sometimes circumstances don't give you time to ask such questions. An unexpected illness might give you days (or at most, weeks) to consider these issues; an accident or injury might leave you with hours, or even minutes. Whenever possible, however, it's best to develop a plan, taking into consideration three basic issues:

1) **When should you consider euthanasia?** When your pet is ill, this may be the last question you want to think about. Yet it is the most important question you may need to answer.

Start by asking your veterinarian what types of symptoms to expect as your pet's illness progresses. What stages will the disease take? How long before kidney disease produces incontinence or renal failure? How long before tumor cells invade the lungs or other organs? How long before symptoms become medically unmanageable, before pain becomes severe and untreatable? At what point will your pet become unable to function normally; at what point will its suffering become extreme?

This information can help you form your plan. For example, you may decide to seriously consider euthanasia when your pet can no longer breathe easily, or eat or drink, or find a comfortable position in which to sleep, or when it seems to find your touch painful. By defining a "decision point" in advance, you place boundaries on the suffering your pet is likely to endure.

2) **Will you be there?** Many people feel it is important to be present during euthanasia. Many others feel unable to handle this traumatic event. And make no mistake: Witnessing the euthanasia of your beloved companion IS traumatic (though it can also help allay fears that your companion suffered). This is not a decision to be made lightly, or based on someone else's choices.

Most feel that the pet's well-being is the most important consideration. If you believe your pet will feel more comfortable or secure in your presence, you'll probably want to stay, no matter how difficult it will be. On the other hand, if you're concerned that your own reaction and grief may disturb the pet more than the process itself, you may prefer to stay away.

If you choose not to be present, don't simply leave your pet with the veterinarian. Some clinics hold "to-be-euthanized" pets until after clinic hours, which simply add to an animal's trauma. Make sure that your pet is going to be euthanized immediately, while you wait in the waiting room or car.

3) **What will you do next?** The worst time to decide what to do with your pet's remains is at the last minute. It's far better to begin discussing options weeks in advance. Indeed, even the owner of a perfectly healthy pet can begin considering the answer to this question at any time, particularly if you want to make special funeral or private cremation arrangements, or want a particular type of funerary product (such as a special urn or casket).

For many, this decision involves both physical and spiritual issues. How do you (and your family) distinguish between body and soul? Do you feel that your pet will be "closer" to you spiritually if its remains are close to you physically (e.g., in a cremation urn)? Do you feel that your pet's spirit will be happier if it is interred in a familiar, beloved location? Or do you feel that your pet's soul and personality are not associated with its physical remains, which you're quite happy to leave with the veterinarian? There's nothing foolish about such considerations. For many, the certainty that they have provided for their cat's spiritual needs can go a long way toward healing the spiritual wounds of the owner.

Myths About Euthanasia

Many people have mixed feelings about euthanasia, for good reason. No matter how well-intentioned we may be, this act feels like murder to many of us, and guilt may often haunt us long after the act.

Even when we know intellectually that euthanasia may be the "best" or "most merciful" choice, that means little when we face the decision itself. Many pet owners cling to misperceptions that provide apparent justification for postponing this decision—often at the expense of the pet itself. Three common misperceptions include:

1) **Euthanasia isn't nature's way.** Some pet owners reject euthanasia as "unnatural." Nature, some say, has a timetable for every life, and by artificially ending a life, we're disrupting nature's plan. While charming, this belief overlooks the fact that by providing treatment, surgery, medication, or any other form of care for a sick (or injured) pet, we are already extending that pet's life far beyond what would ocur if matters were left in the not-so-tender hands of "nature." Euthanasia is often not so much a question of "artificially ending" a life, but of determining when to cease artificially extending that life.

2) **Euthanasia is selfish.** One of the commonest sources of guilt is the belief that one has euthanized a pet "too soon" or for "selfish" reasons. "I should have tried harder," many tell themselves. "I should have been willing to do more, spend more, get a second opinion, stay up all night to take care of her." Yet the person who worries most about not having "done enough" is often a person who has already gone to superhuman efforts to care for that pet. A far more dangerous form of selfishness is to prolong a pet's suffering simply to postpone one's own.

3) **My pet will tell me when it's "time."** Many of us have heard of pets who allegedly offered some indication of acceptance of death, of being "ready to move on." And who among us would not welcome that sense of being granted "permission" to end a pet's life? Such a "signal" would remove the dreadful burden of having to make that decision on our own. Unfortunately, for many that signal never comes. By convincing ourselves that our pets will "tell us" when it is time to die, we risk two hazards: Prolonging a pet's suffering by waiting for a sign that never comes, or torturing ourselves with guilt for acting "too soon."

The painful truth is that if your pet is terminally ill, and especially if it is suffering and unable to function, it will die; the decision you must make is not whether its life will end, but how, and how much discomfort you are willing to allow it to endure. Stefanie Schwartz, DVM, sums up the issue in one vital question in her book, Canine and Feline Behavior Problems: "Which choice will bring you the least cause for regret after the pet is gone?" Unfortunately, "no regret" is often not an option.

EUTHANASIA:
HOW WILL I KNOW WHEN IT'S TIME?

By Marcia Breitenbach

Pippin needed assistance from his owner to get to his feet. He slowly walked to the door, then needed help once again to step down onto the back porch. With a slight groan, he squatted to relieve himself and came back towards the house. There was no twinkle in his eye, and this time he needed to be carried all the way back to his bed. He'd used up his energy for that day.

I got a call from Pippin's owner that day asking me, "Do you think it's time for me to put him down?" This wasn't the first time Pippin's owner had asked me this question, nor was it the first time I'd faced this dilemma with others. As the facilitator of a pet loss group, I had sat with many who were grieving and reliving the pain of this situation.

For almost everyone who came to this group who had used euthanasia to assist their animal companions to 'the other side,' there was either the fear that they had waited too long or that they had done it too soon. Each person doubted that they had gotten it right.

Every now and then, I would run across someone who didn't carry this guilt or doubt. I learned from them what had helped them to find clarity and peace with their decision. So, as I spoke to Pippin's owner that day, I was careful in what I chose to say, knowing that this decision would affect the person's grief journey, as well as their confidence and self-esteem.

Here are some helpful reminders for making your decision:

1) YOU ARE THE EXPERT concerning your animal's care. No one knows them better than you. Gather information to the best of your ability to help you in making this decision.

2) Euthanasia may seem unnatural to some. Consider that "nature" is defied every day as sick animals have their lives prolonged by surgeries, medicines and procedures that aren't necessarily "natural."

3) Asking others for input can be helpful, and it can also derail you. Be careful who you ask and what you ask. If you are going to ask your vet their opinion, let them know that you will be making this decision and would like them to give you compassionate feedback, not a lecture or a "you must do this my way" recommendation. Pay particular attention to their knowledge about the signposts that indicate your animal is suffering and what to expect in terms of medical management.

4) Ask your animal. So many people are afraid to do this. They say, "I'm no Dr. Doolittle. I can't talk to them." This is untrue. We all communicate with our animals a lot more than we know. Much of it may not catch our attention because we are so used to it. They put their thoughts into our minds, as we do with our thoughts and words to them. All it takes is some quiet and stillness.

Take a pen and some paper and sit quietly with your animal. Do some stretching and deep breathing to relax your body. Shut your eyes and have the intention or say a short prayer to be connected with your animal's mind and heart. Say (silently) what you would like to your pet—perhaps something like, "I can see that your body is losing strength and having a hard time. I sense that your time to let go of your physical body is coming closer. I am so sad about this, as I will miss you very much. You have brought such joy and love to my life. And I love you so much that I don't want you to suffer during this transition.

Could you tell me, in some way, whether you would like assistance with this process? Are you ready to go?" After you say what is in your heart, you must sit still and keep your mind and heart open. Feel a band of light going from your pet's heart to your own. After a period of time, at least ten minutes, open your eyes and write down thoughts, images or feelings you had during that time. Trust your perceptions as more than a vivid imagination.

5) More and more people will call an animal communicator or pet psychic to speak with the animal. This can be very helpful. Know ahead of time, if you can, whom you will call and that you can trust their perceptions. Ask your veterinarian or friends for recommendations.

6) If you feel you haven't received any useful information, then ask yourself, "Which choice will I have less regrets about when this is over?"

7) Sometimes our pets stay longer because they are worried about us, about whether we will be ok when they are gone. Have a talk with them and let them know that it is ok to go when they are ready, that you will be ok. Tell them that you will grieve their absence, but that you will reach out to others for support. Sometimes, just getting this permission from you allows them to die without the assistance of euthanasia.

8) If you do decide to euthanize, don't do it alone. Have a friend or family member accompany you. If you want to be with your animal at the time of the injection, make sure you do it in a way that minimizes trauma to you both. Dim the lights if you can. Have a favorite blanket with you that your pet is cradled in. Speak to them again and tell them of your love and gratitude for being part of your life and that you will always be connected…that you will see them again…whatever is in your heart in that moment.

If s/he is in your arms, you may want to consider holding the animal so that you are not gazing into their eyes. It is a personal choice, but one that can make your grief harder. Many people say they are haunted by what they felt were painful "why?" or other critical questions in the pet's eyes as they died. This is most likely projection of the human's confusion and guilt, rather than the animal's confusion.

9) Decide in advance how to handle the body. Some cities have pet cemeteries that will cremate or bury your pet's body. Having a memorial service for family and close friends can assist the natural process of grief.

Even with these tips to help you, know that grief for an animal companion is still hard work, just as it is for loss of a human companion. Give yourself permission to grieve, to remember the precious times with them, and know that you made the best choice you could in your particular moment. There are no right or wrong choices here. Take comfort knowing that your beloved animal wasn't and isn't judging you. Their love is unconditional and, as the great spiritual teachers that they are, they are holding you in their hearts, wherever they may be, wishing for you a happy, guilt-free and purposeful life.

Marcia Breitenbach is an author, musician, expressive arts grief therapist, and presenter. Visit her at http://www.griefandlosshelp.com

THE FINAL FAREWELL:
HOW TO HANDLE A PET'S REMAINS

by Moira Anderson Allen, M.Ed.

In other articles, I've talked about the most painful decision a pet owner ever has to face—the decision about whether, or when, to euthanize a pet. But the death of a pet brings with it yet another difficult decision, and one which you may not be prepared, at the moment of loss, to deal with. That is the decision of how to handle your pet's remains.

Many pet owners never even think about this issue until their vet suddenly asks, "What do you want to do with the body?" Needless to say, this is not the best time to think calmly and rationally about all the options available and arrive at a well-thought-out decision. Unfortunately, this often leads to a hasty decision made at the height of painful emotion—and a decision that one may later regret.

The only alternative is to consider this decision ahead of time. Asking yourself what you want to do with your pet's remains while that pet is still alive and healthy isn't ghoulish. It's a responsible way of facing, and dealing with, a painful reality. It also gives you an opportunity to evaluate all the factors that may be involved in such a decision.

The first factor to consider is your own feelings about death, loss, and remembrance. When you face the death of a pet, your goal will be to preserve the memory of that pet—and your decision should be based on how you think that memory can be best preserved.

Funerals: The Final Farewell

Many people feel that providing a dignified burial or cremation for a pet is a final, fitting act of farewell. They feel that it is the last act of love that they can offer a pet, and it is also, quite often, an important act of closure. Actually being able to view, touch, and say farewell to a pet's body can help one accept that the pet is really dead, that it is not going to come back— and also that it is not suffering in any way. If it is important to you to see that your pet's remains are treated with the same concern and care that you gave your pet during its life, then you should look into home burial, pet cemetery burial, or cremation through a pet crematory. Here's a closer look at these options:

1) Home Burial. Many people choose to bury a pet at home as a way of keeping it close—a part of one's world, even if it isn't a part of one's life. This can also provide a way for you and your family to celebrate a funeral and memorial service, which in themselves can be powerful coping tools. Some pet owners have also reported that their surviving pets seem to understand that their companion is still "present", and report that those pets may spend time visiting the gravesite. Home burial provides the opportunity to create a permanent memorial to one's pet—a grave marker, a statue, or perhaps a tree planted over the pet's grave to serve as a living memorial. (Others choose to bury a pet under an existing shrub or tree that the pet liked to sleep under.)

In some circumstances, however, home burial may not be an appropriate option. The most obvious is if you have no place in which to bury a pet. You must also be sure that you can dig a deep enough grave to ensure that your pet's remains will not be disturbed or become a health hazard. (Don't bury a pet in a flowerbed that is likely to be redug and replanted.) Many cities prohibit home burials. You also might not wish to bury a pet at home if you rent, or if you are likely to move away from the property.

2) Cremation. If you would still like to keep your pet's remains on your property, but don't have a place to bury an actual body (especially that of a large pet), consider having your pet's remains cremated and returned to you for burial. This still has the advantage of keeping your pet "at home," but bypasses health problems or the concern that the pet's remains might be disturbed later. Or, you can keep the pet's ashes in a decorative urn or container; you'll find a wide range of such products in the classified ads of any pet magazine.

Many pet owners choose to scatter a pet's ashes rather than preserve them. Some choose to scatter the ashes in the pet's own yard, where it lived and played; this is another way of bringing the pet "home" one last time. Others choose to scatter the ashes in a way that symbolizes setting the pet "free" for its final journey—such as in the woods or over a body of water, or just into the wind. Pet crematories can now be found in many cities; a pet crematory can usually pick up your pet's remains from a veterinarian or from your home. Some veterinarians also provide cremation services; some will do so at no extra charge if they have euthanized your pet or if it dies at the vet's office. (Not all veterinarians provide this service, so it might be advisable to check this in advance.)

3) Cemetery Burial. You'll find pet cemeteries in nearly every state; some have literally dozens. For many, a formal cemetery burial seems a more fitting tribute than an informal "backyard burial". Burial in a pet cemetery also ensures that your pet's remains will remain undisturbed, and cared for, "in perpetuity." You will not have to worry about what will happen to your pet if you have to leave the property on which it is buried; it will be cared for, no matter where you go or what happens to you. Cemetery burial can be a costly option, but many find it a comforting, secure way to handle a pet's remains. A pet cemetery will usually be able to pick up your pet from your home or from a veterinarian's office. If you wish, you can make arrangements for a complete funeral and memorial service.

It's the Spirit, Not the Body

While some pet owners feel very strongly about the need to provide a proper resting place for a pet's body, others feel that the body is merely the receptacle for the pet's spirit. When that spirit is gone, many view the body as simply an abandoned shell, with little meaning of its own. Such owners are generally more concerned with preserving the memory of a pet and honoring its spirit and its life, than with fussing over its remains. Some even feel that there's something a bit gruesome about keeping the physical remains of a pet (such as its ashes) around after the pet has "gone." Many also believe that the expense of having a pet formally cremated, or interred in a pet cemetery, would be put to better use providing for the needs of a living pet.

If this describes you, then the question of convenience may play a central role in your decision. If your pet dies or is euthanized at a veterinarian's office, you may prefer to simply allow the vet to dispose of its remains. If your pet dies at home, you may wish to bury it at home not so much out of sentiment, but because it may be simpler than finding someone else to handle disposal. (Most vets will not charge for the disposal of a pet that dies in the vet's office, but will charge if the pet has died elsewhere.)

If you do not have a location in which to bury a pet, but do not wish to pay any disposal fees, one option is to take your pet to your local humane society. Most humane societies are set up to receive and dispose of animal remains, and most do not charge. Some even have "drop off" bins—though most pet owners regard this as being a bit too much like dumping a pet into the trash.

A Family Decision

Before you make any decision about how to dispose of a pet, make sure that you have considered the feelings and beliefs (and needs) of all family members. You may find that while one family member feels that a pet's body means little after the spirit has gone, another may feel strongly about the need to provide a formal "farewell" in the form of a burial. Conversely, you may find that while some members of the family want a formal burial service, others shudder at the thought of having a grave or "dead body" in the yard.

It is important to realize that there is no right or wrong viewpoint in such a discussion. One's feelings about death, and about the remains of the dead, are intensely personal—and in a family discussion about how to handle those remains, everyone's feelings should be respected. This is why it is so important to raise this issue and resolve it before a pet dies. Otherwise, chances are that one family member (i.e., whoever is present when a pet dies or is euthanized) will have to make a rushed, emotional decision that may not be the decision the rest of the family would have chosen.

It's not easy to talk about a pet's death, or use terms like "remains" and "disposal", while that pet is still alive and very much a part of the family. But avoiding the subject isn't going to prevent the problem from coming up. It's simply going to prevent you from being in a position to handle it effectively when it does come up.

It has been said that "funerals are for the living." When a pet dies, you're faced with the need to make a decision that can have a profound impact on how you, and your family, deal with that loss. Don't leave that decision until the last minute.

Author's Note: Since this article was posted, several readers have reminded me to mention that if you choose to leave your pet's body with a veterinarian or humane society for disposal, you may not have a choice in how that body is disposed of. If you wish to ensure that your pet is, in fact, cremated, be sure to request this option. If the option is not available, you will need to take your pet's remains elsewhere.

One other factor to consider is that if your pet dies in such a way that its remains are collected by your local city or county animal control agency (e.g., your pet is hit by a car and found on the road by the authorities, or, in one person's tragic situation, is found by firefighters in a house fire), you may have no control over how these authorities dispose of the body. Such authorities are not equipped to "hold" a pet's remains for the owner to claim.

Grieving

Grief

is a journey

with no road map.

There is no right or wrong way to do it

nor is there a time schedule for it.

One day along that journey,

you begin to discover that

some of the tears

begin to turn to smiles

as we remember

all the good and funny times.

from Dogster Member: Wyoming

Dogs are not our whole life,
but they make our lives whole.

—Roger Caras

MY GRIEVING

I cried at the thought of losing Abby.

I cried when the Vet came to help Abby with her final journey home.

I cried when Abby was gone.

Then, in the words of one of my favorite Pink Floyd songs, I became comfortably numb.

I couldn't handle the tears any more, so I cut them off. Abby's photo is on my desktop, and I stopped looking at it. If I didn't cry, then I wouldn't feel the pain. What I didn't understand was that feeling the pain is a necessary part of grieving. And I wouldn't get past the grieving until I let all the tears out. At times it felt like an avalanche, a tsunami of tears. Where did they all come from? Was there some huge tear bag in my tummy that just stored all these tears, waiting to pour them out? I'm learning now that it's not good for me to repress all these emotions, to hold back all these tears. Every one grieves differently, for different times, in different ways. There is no normal in grieving.

Without a doubt, the death of a pet is a traumatic experience. It's not just a dog; it's like a family member. And sometimes, society downplays our pet's role in society. You can't take time off work to grieve the loss of a pet without people thinking that to be strange. I'm learning that grief has to be expressed, no matter how painful it is.

PET LOSS:
UNDERSTANDING GRIEF IN CHILDREN

When an adult loses a beloved pet, grief is a normal reaction. It progresses through very predictable stages which have been defined as denial, sadness, depression, guilt, anger, and finally, relief (or recovery). The effect of grief and loss on children is less predictable and depends upon the child's age and maturity level. The capacity of children to understand death dictates their response to the experience of grief and loss.

Death and dying are two of the hardest facts of life to explain to children. Very often, the death of a family pet is a child's first encounter with this immutable law of nature. How we handle this event can have a far-reaching impact on our children's understanding of death and dying.

Under Two

A child can feel and respond to a pet's death, based on the reaction of those around him or her. A child picks up the stress felt by family members, no matter what the cause.

Two and Three Year Old Children

Young children typically have no life experiences upon which to draw when they face the loss of a pet. They may consider it a form of sleep. They should be told that their pet has died and will not return.

Two and three year old children should be reassured that the pet's absence is unrelated to anything the child may have said or done. Usually, a child in this age range will easily accept another pet in place of the dead one. Although the child may be unaware of the concept of death, stress in the household can be detected. It is advisable to stick to routines and provide care and reassurance for the young child.

Four, Five, and Six Year Old Children

Children in this age range have some understanding of death but in a way that relates to a continued existence. The pet may be considered to be living underground while continuing to eat, breathe, and play. The child will miss the animal as a playmate, but not necessarily as a love object. They will see death as a temporary state—something like the way leaves fall off a tree in fall but grow back in the spring. Alternatively, he may be considered asleep. A return to life may be expected if the child views death as temporary. Some television cartoons may suggest to children that it is possible to return from death.

These children often feel that any anger they had toward the pet may be responsible for his death. This view should be discouraged because they may also translate this belief to the death of family members. Some children also see death as contagious and begin to fear that their own death (or that of others) is imminent. They should be reassured that their death is not likely.

As they perceive the trauma around them, they may regress in their behavior. Manifestations of grief may take the form of alterations in bladder and bowel control, eating habits, and sleeping. The child should be encouraged to talk with the parent and voice concerns about what has happened. In this age group, a few brief discussions may be more productive than one or two lengthy sessions.

Seven, Eight, and Nine Year Old Children

Children in this age group know that death is irreversible and they are capable of intense grief. They usually do not personalize death, thinking it cannot happen to them. However, some children may develop concerns about death of their parents. They may become very curious about death and ask questions that, on the surface, appear morbid. These questions are natural and parents should respond frankly and honestly.

Grief may be expressed in a variety of ways. Problems may arise at school with learning and behavior. Interpersonal skills with adults and peers may deteriorate. In rare cases, grief-related anxiety may be expressed through acts of aggression. Additionally, withdrawal, neediness or clinging behavior may be seen. Parents should remain alert and attentive, as the difficulties may not arise for several weeks, or even months.

This is also the period when children recognize a correlation between what they think and what happens. For instance, a child may resent taking care

of the pet and wish—however briefly—that the pet would die. If the pet then dies, the child is often consumed with guilt. Parents need to reassure children that they did not cause the pet's death.

Ten and Eleven Year Old Children

Children in this age range are usually able to understand that death is natural, inevitable, and universal. They generally understand that all living things will eventually die, and that death is total. Understanding and accepting are two different things, however. They may go through the normal stages of grief that grownups do: denial, bargaining, anger, guilt, depression and acceptance. Or they may react in other ways:

Depending on the age, the child may regress (sucking their thumb or temper tantrums that they had outgrown).

An older child may withdraw from friends and family for a while. Schoolwork may suffer and they may seem uninterested in extracurricular activities.

Children may fear abandonment. If a pet can die, then they may reason that their parents could die as well.

Children often become intensely curious about death and what happens to the body. They may ask for details that you may find uncomfortable to explain. These are questions you should answer in a straightforward, gentle and careful manner.

Adolescents

Although this age group also reacts similarly to adults, many adolescents may exhibit various forms of denial. This may take the form of a total lack of emotion. They may also act out their pain through antisocial acts. Adults should not expect the grief process to follow a particular time-frame with teenagers. Because the teenage years are fraught with excess emotion, some situations require that the parent offer as much reassurance about pet death as would be given to a young child.

Young Adults

Loss of a pet can be particularly hard at this age, especially if the pet has been a family member for many years. Some psychologists say that, in effect, loss of such a pet represents a "rite of passage" to adulthood. Young adults need the same opportunities to voice their feelings as any of the other age groups.

Summary

Professional bereavement counselors are available in most cities. Do not be afraid to seek professional advice if you have questions about the experience of grief and pet loss. The normal balance in a family can be so disrupted that, occasionally, it is helpful to solicit outside assistance.

EXPLAINING PET LOSS TO CHILDREN: DO'S AND DON'TS

The worst course of action is to lie (to say the animal went away) or to use confusing euphemisms, such as the phrase "put to sleep." Children will eventually learn the truth, and lying can breed resentment and destroy trust between parent and child. Later in life, when the child learns the truth, they'll wonder what else the parent lied about.

Likewise, euphemisms can cause anxiety or confusion because children take what you say literally. If you say a pet is put to sleep, the child may suffer sleep anxiety. For example, a child who was told his cocker spaniel just "went away" may await his dog's return, and upon learning the dog had been buried want to unearth the dog. If you say 'God has taken your pet because he was special,' the child may resent God, and fear who might be next.

- Be open and honest. This includes the pet's health and euthanasia. If a pet is terminally ill and needs to be euthanized, the child needs to be told as soon as possible by the parent. Again, avoid those tempting euphemisms that cloud understanding, such as telling a child the pet was put to sleep. Use the words death and dying to make your meaning clear. Telling a child that their pet was "put to sleep" can result in the child fearing their own sleep for fear of not waking up.

Some children want to be present during euthanasia and most will be very curious about the process. Always answer their questions with age appropriate, honest responses. As for allowing the child to be present, it depends on the child's age and maturity. Most importantly, it depends on whether the child understands what is happening and whether or not they want to be there.

- Make sure the child understands what "dying" means. Explain that the animal's body stopped working. Depending on your religious beliefs and what the child can understand, you might explain the concept of a soul. However, it is important for the child to know that the pet has died and will not be coming back.

- Be available to let your child discuss his/her feelings about what happened. You may want to hold your own service to memorialize the pet and to say goodbye formally. Some people plant trees in a special spot in the yard, others bury the pet in a cemetery so the family can visit. Encourage your child to show his/her feelings by talking or writing about the fun times they had with their pet. Younger children may want to send a letter or photo to "heaven" with them. Sometimes, a photo may be taken of the pet with their letter prior to the pet's death. This aids children in knowing that they were a part of their life and death and that they did not fail their companion in any way.

- Show your own feelings. This tells the child that the pet was special and that they are not grieving alone. You can also encourage your child to open up, which can help the healing process. How a family models feelings after the death of a pet may largely determine how future difficult feelings are expressed.

- Tell your child's teachers about the loss, so they will understand why your child is behaving differently.

- Don't blame the veterinarian. Some parents, especially those who fear explaining euthanasia to their children, find it easier to lay it all on the vet. This is not only unfair to the veterinarian, but potentially harmful to the child. He or she may grow up distrusting veterinarians and, by extension, doctors and other medical professionals.

In addition, parents shouldn't throw the responsibility of telling the children what needs to be done on the veterinarian. Your veterinarian can help the parent explain why euthanasia may be the most humane option, and answer questions the child may have.

Parents often want to ease their child's hurt by rushing out and buying another pet. This is a mistake. The last thing you want to do is convey the impression that the pet—a family member—is replaceable. Wait until the child expresses an interest in another pet.

Children are very resilient, and they usually learn to accept their pet is gone. If a child persists with nightmares or seems unable to cope, however, it may be necessary to talk with a counselor.

Where to Turn for Help

There are a number of organizations dedicated to helping people cope around the country. To find one in your state, visit the Delta Society Web page at www.deltasociety.org.

I think dogs are the most amazing creatures.
They give unconditional love.
For me, they are the role model
for being alive.

—*Gilda Radner*

PET BEREAVEMENT

Trish Lane

Shiva's Center for the Human-Animal Bond is a not-for-profit organization founded in 2006 by Dr. Trish Lane, psychologist. Dr. Lane moved to Santa Barbara in 2002 to help establish the California Animal Referral & Emergency Hospital. The hospital was dedicated to Shiva, Dr. Lane's canine companion who died in 2003. The name of the not-for-profit Lane subsequently established would also honor Shiva and reflect the general purpose of the organization "Shiva's Center for the Human-Animal Bond."

At the time of Shiva's death, Santa Barbara did not offer any pet loss support groups. Having previously identified the need, one of the first goals of Shiva's Center was the formation of free pet bereavement groups. Honoring the loss of animal companions is one way we recognize the importance of the human-animal bond. The human-animal bond refers to that strong positive interaction that exists between humans and animals—the special bond that enhances human quality of life.

The loss of the human-animal bond often results in grief. Grief can be described as emotions and behavior that ensue when a love relationship has ended. The closeness of the love relationship will be predictive of the intensity of the loss. In the context of the human-animal bond, individuals value the relationship regardless of species. In addition, grief may be compounded by the lack of support or understanding about the significance of the loss.

It's not unusual for individuals to share that losing their pet was more painful than losing a close family member. Despite their experience of loss, many are ridiculed, teased, or have their feelings dismissed and so choose to hide their intense pain. One man shares, "Don't tell me he was 'just a dog,' he was my best friend. Don't ask me if I've gotten over it yet; I'll never get over him." A woman describes her boss's thoughtlessness, "It's just a cat—you can get another one at the pound for fifty bucks." Her response, "If my husband died or my home burned down, I could get another one of them as well—it's about the relationship and I loved my cat just as much if not more." Unfortunately, it's not uncommon for these attitudes to come from family members, friends, colleagues, and employers. Even therapists have been reported to have made such hurtful remarks. As people are educated about the human-animal bond the goal is that they will come to have a greater appreciation for the relationship.

Having the choice of euthanasia presents a difficult dilemma for individuals. There is no real comparison with the loss of loved humans, because we do not euthanize human beings. Nothing seems to complicate the grief process like the guilt that may accompany the responsibility of ending the life of a dear friend that you have loved and nurtured. Having noted this, it seems that guilt is the biggest hurdle for people to handle. Although euthanasia literally means "good death", nothing good comes with the responsibility of this decision. Many individuals who elect to euthanize are often stuck in the "what if's" and need considerable guidance to make peace with their decision. Group support can be a powerful healer as members may forgive themselves as they forgive one another. Sometimes, it is through this sharing that people come to trust their decision. Alternately, it helps to simply ask them if their pet would want them to be experiencing so much psychological pain. Inevitably, the answer is "no."

Similar to adults, children undoubtedly need support, guidance, and information. Naturally, the same principles of the human-animal bond hold true for children. Research has demonstrated that if children are old enough to feel, they are old enough to grieve. The loss of a pet is most often a child's first experience of death. And children typically identify the loss of a pet as the saddest experience of their life.

NORMAL GRIEF RESPONSE
AFTER THE DEATH OF YOUR PET

Reasons why it may hurt so much when a pet dies

- Your pet is a source of unconditional love and appreciation

- A pet becomes part of who you are; An alter-ego, child and/or companion

- Many times, places, feelings, thoughts and events are associated with your pet

- Your pet did things just for you and you did things just for your pet

- Each of you gave the other a great deal of emotional support

- Losing your pet is like losing a part of yourself

What you might feel after the death

- Shock/numbness

- Denial

- Anger/guilt

- Regret

- Relief

- Depression

What you may experience physically

- Crying

- Dry mouth, difficulty in swallowing

- No appetite or over-eating

- Sleep disturbances

- Aching heart, chest pains and/or an empty, hollow feeling

- Lack of energy and motivation

- Unable to concentrate, forgetfulness

- Sensitivity to loud noises

What you may experience emotionally

- Everything reminds you of your pet, you may experience seeing or hearing your pet

- Feeling distanced from others, as if no one understands or cares

- Questioning the meaning of life and mortality, re-evaluating your priorities in life

- Worrying about others you love dying

- Afraid to love again, fear of the pain of loss

The labor of mourning

It is called the labor of mourning because it is exhausting and difficult work to grieve over the loss of a loved one. The "work" is actually feeling the pain that you experience whenever you think of or are reminded of your pet who is no longer with you. Healthy grieving is going through the pain. It is a typical response to try avoiding the pain. In the long run that may make things worse. The pain of the loss will soften in time if you acknowledge it. Yes, pain hurts and it is uncomfortable, but it is not bad—it is a testimony of the love and joy you shared with your pet.

What helps soften the pain

- Talking, talking... To family, friends, co-workers, a support group and/or counselor

- Writing about your pet and about your feelings in a journal

- Creating a funeral /memorial service, sharing memories, sharing your pain

- Be extra kind to yourself; Get a massage, a bubble bath, exercise, visit with friends

- Set up a memorial in your pet's honor. Create a ritual, and repeat it every year.

TEN TIPS ON COPING WITH PET LOSS

by Moira Anderson Allen, M.Ed.

Anyone who considers a pet a beloved friend, companion, or family member knows the intense pain that accompanies the loss of that friend. Following are some tips on coping with that grief, and with the difficult decisions one faces upon the loss of a pet.

1. Am I crazy to hurt so much?

Intense grief over the loss of a pet is normal and natural. Don't let anyone tell you that it's silly, crazy, or overly sentimental to grieve!

During the years you spent with your pet (even if they were few), it became a significant and constant part of your life. It was a source of comfort and companionship, of unconditional love and acceptance, of fun and joy. So don't be surprised if you feel devastated by the loss of such a relationship.

People who don't understand the pet/owner bond may not understand your pain. All that matters, however, is how you feel. Don't let others dictate your feelings: They are valid, and may be extremely painful. But remember, you are not alone: Thousands of pet owners have gone through the same feelings.

2. What Can I Expect to Feel?

Different people experience grief in different ways. Besides your sorrow and loss, you may also experience the following emotions:

- Guilt may occur if you feel responsible for your pet's death—the "if only I had been more careful" syndrome. It is pointless and often erroneous to burden yourself with guilt for the accident or illness that claimed your pet's life, and only makes it more difficult to resolve your grief.

- Denial makes it difficult to accept that your pet is really gone. It's hard to imagine that your pet won't greet you when you come home, or that it doesn't need its evening meal. Some pet owners carry this to extremes, and fear their pet is still alive and suffering somewhere. Others find it hard to get a new pet for fear of being "disloyal" to the old.

- Anger may be directed at the illness that killed your pet, the driver of the speeding car, the veterinarian who "failed" to save its life. Sometimes it is justified, but when carried to extremes, it distracts you from the important task of resolving your grief.

- Depression is a natural consequence of grief, but can leave you powerless to cope with your feelings. Extreme depression robs you of motivation and energy, causing you to dwell upon your sorrow.

3. What can I do about my feelings?

The most important step you can take is to be honest about your feelings. Don't deny your pain, or your feelings of anger and guilt. Only by examining and coming to terms with your feelings can you begin to work through them.

You have a right to feel pain and grief! Someone you loved has died, and you feel alone and bereaved. You have a right to feel anger and guilt, as well. Acknowledge your feelings first, then ask yourself whether the circumstances actually justify them.

Locking away grief doesn't make it go away. Express it. Cry, scream, pound the floor, talk it out. Do what helps you the most. Don't try to avoid grief by not thinking about your pet; instead, reminisce about the good times. This will help you understand what your pet's loss actually means to you.

Some find it helpful to express their feelings and memories in poems, stories, or letters to the pet. Other strategies including rearranging your schedule to fill in the times you would have spent with your pet; preparing a memorial such as a photo collage; and talking to others about your loss.

4. Who can I talk to?

If your family or friends love pets, they'll understand what you're going through. Don't hide your feelings in a misguided effort to appear strong and calm! Working through your feelings with another person is one of the best ways to put them in perspective and find ways to handle them. Find someone you can talk to about how much the pet meant to you and how much you miss it—someone you feel comfortable crying and grieving with.

If you don't have family or friends who understand, or if you need more help, ask your veterinarian or humane association to recommend a pet loss counselor or support group. Check with your church or hospital for grief counseling. Remember, your grief is genuine and deserving of support.

5. When is the right time to euthanize a pet?

Your veterinarian is the best judge of your pet's physical condition; however, you are the best judge of the quality of your pet's daily life. If a pet has a good appetite, responds to attention, seeks its owner's company, and participates in play or family life, many owners feel that this is not the time. However, if a pet is in constant pain, undergoing difficult and stressful treatments that aren't helping greatly, unresponsive to affection, unaware of its surroundings, and uninterested in life, a caring pet owner will probably choose to end the beloved companion's suffering.

Evaluate your pet's health honestly and unselfishly with your veterinarian. Prolonging a pet's suffering in order to prevent your own ultimately helps neither of you. Nothing can make this decision an easy or painless one, but it is truly the final act of love that you can make for your pet.

6. Should I stay during euthanasia?

Many feel this is the ultimate gesture of love and comfort you can offer your pet. Some feel relief and comfort themselves by staying: They were able to see that their pet passed peacefully and without pain, and that it was truly gone. For many, not witnessing the death (and not seeing the body) makes it more difficult to accept that the pet is really gone. However, this can be traumatic, and you must ask yourself honestly whether you will be able to handle it. Uncontrolled emotions and tears-though natural-are likely to upset your pet.

Some clinics are more open than others to allowing the owner to stay during euthanasia. Some veterinarians are also willing to euthanize a pet at home. Others have come to an owner's car to administer the injection. Again, consider what will be least traumatic for you and your pet, and discuss your desires and concerns with your veterinarian. If your clinic is not able to accommodate your wishes, request a referral.

7. What do I do next?

When a pet dies, you must choose how to handle its remains. Sometimes, in the midst of grief, it may seem easiest to leave the pet at the clinic for disposal. Check with your clinic to find out whether there is a fee for such disposal. Some shelters also accept such remains, though many charge a fee for disposal.

If you prefer a more formal option, several are available. Home burial is a popular choice, if you have sufficient property for it. It is economical and enables you to design your own funeral ceremony at little cost. However, city regulations usually prohibit pet burials, and this is not a good choice for renters or people who move frequently.

To many, a pet cemetery provides a sense of dignity, security, and permanence. Owners appreciate the serene surroundings and care of the gravesite. Cemetery costs vary depending on the services you select, as well as upon the type of pet you have. Cremation is a less expensive option that allows you to handle your pet's remains in a variety of ways: bury them (even in the city), scatter them in a favorite location, place them in a columbarium, or even keep them with you in a decorative urn (of which a wide variety are available).

Check with your veterinarian, pet shop, or phone directory for options available in your area. Consider your living situation, personal and religious values, finances, and future plans when making your decision. It's also wise to make such plans in advance, rather than hurriedly in the midst of grief.

8. What should I tell my children?

You are the best judge of how much information your children can handle about death and the loss of their pet. Don't underestimate them, however. You may find that, by being honest with them about your pet's loss, you may be able to address some fears and misperceptions they have about death.

Honesty is important. If you say the pet was "put to sleep," make sure your children understand the difference between death and ordinary sleep. Never say the pet "went away," or your child may wonder what he or she did to make it leave, and wait in anguish for its return. That also makes it harder for a child to accept a new pet. Make it clear that the pet will not come back, but that it is happy and free of pain.

Never assume a child is too young or too old to grieve. Never criticize a child for tears, or tell them to "be strong" or not to feel sad. Be honest about your own sorrow; don't try to hide it, or children may feel required to hide their grief as well. Discuss the issue with the entire family, and give everyone a chance to work through their grief at their own pace.

9. Will my other pets grieve?

Pets observe every change in a household, and are bound to notice the absence of a companion. Pets often form strong attachments to one another, and the survivor of such a pair may seem to grieve for its companion. Cats grieve for dogs, and dogs for cats.

You may need to give your surviving pets a lot of extra attention and love to help them through this period. Remember that, if you are going to introduce a new pet, your surviving pets may not accept the newcomer right away, but new bonds will grow in time. Meanwhile, the love of your surviving pets can be wonderfully healing for your own grief.

10. Should I get a new pet right away?

Generally, the answer is no. One needs time to work through grief and loss before attempting to build a relationship with a new pet. If your emotions are still in turmoil, you may resent a new pet for trying to "take the place" of the old-for what you really want is your old pet back. Children in particular may feel that loving a new pet is "disloyal" to the previous pet.

When you do get a new pet, avoid getting a "lookalike" pet, which makes comparisons all the more likely. Don't expect your new pet to be "just like" the one you lost, but allow it to develop its own personality. Never give a new pet the same name or nickname as the old. Avoid the temptation to compare the new pet to the old one: It can be hard to remember that your beloved companion also caused a few problems when it was young!

A new pet should be acquired because you are ready to move forward and build a new relationship—rather than looking backward and mourning your loss. When you are ready, select an animal with whom you can build another long, loving relationship—because this is what having a pet is all about!

Don't cry because it's over.
Smile because it happened.

—*Ted Geisel (Dr. Seuss)*

SAYING GOODBYE…A DEATH IN THE FAMILY

By Marian Silverman, M.S., M.F.T., L.E.P.

When my feline companion, Charlie Boy, died, I was distraught and needed time to recover. As a School Psychologist in Los Angeles schools, I was needed at my school because no subs were available to handle my cases. My supervisor asked what was wrong. I told her the truth. "My cat died." She said, "Bereavement days are only allowed if there is a death in the family." I replied, "But Charlie was a member of the family."

I was not allowed a sick day.

Realizing there was a need to change social attitudes toward pet loss, I began to offer bereavement counseling in my private practice. Many of my clients just needed someone to validate their grief. Most well-meaning friends and family told them, "It's just a cat/dog", or "get another one" as if their beloved friend was replaceable. This advice tended to prolong the depression as it made them feel something was wrong with their sadness and they should get over it as quickly as possible. It also trivialized what to them was a devastating loss.

What they needed most was the knowledge that their feelings were normal. One client confessed that this was worse than the death of her parents. Here are some strategies for coping with your pet's death.

1. Permission to Grieve—You deserve to mourn as deeply as you would the death of any member of your family. This is a profound loss. Learning that you are entitled to grieve for as long as you need to, and being encouraged to feel the pain, will help you heal your broken heart.

2. Memorialize—Plan a small service with close friends only—share photos and stories—light candles. This is a time to honor and validate the relationship you had with your pet.

3. Sacred Space—Set up a corner or a table for your memorabilia; photos, collar and tags, a special toy, candles, a poem, ashes in an urn (if you choose to cremate). This is a place where you can feel your pet's energy and talk to him/her.

4. Cry—Crying is very healing and natural. Cry as often and as long as you need to. You are entitled to mourn.

5. Nurture—Get a massage, go to a spa, get a manicure, pedicure, eat a hot fudge sundae, ..in other words, give yourself a luxury you might not usually have.

6. Exercise and Rest—Take a walk by the shore, or in the woods. Get lots of rest, take naps. Your body and psyche have been injured and need to recover. For a sudden death without warning, you may feel as though you have been hit by a truck. You need recovery time, as with any injury.

7. Avoid Toxins—Stay away from people who do not "get" it, those who try to rush you through this, or tell you to "get over it", or "get another one". People may ask you when you are going to replace the pet. This is toxic. If a child dies, would it be appropriate to ask when they were going to replace the child?

8. Write—This is one of the most valuable tools for recovery. Start writing for 15 minutes a day (or longer). Use long hand. Write it raw and rough. Do not edit or be concerned about grammar or spelling. You can do that later if you want to. For now, just write it. Put in all the details, be specific. Write about the death of your pet when you are able to. Read it aloud. Share it with someone you trust with your deepest feelings.

9. Pet Loss Groups and Books—Reach out to support groups. You are not alone in this. Many people are suffering silently and need to talk with others who understand their feelings. A highly recommended book is Goodbye Friend by Gary Kowalski. Check out Amazon.com for other listings.

10. Guilt—Everyone feels it. If only I had done this, or that, or not waited so long, or waited longer, or not left the door open, or changed vets—If Only… Know that you did the very best you could. That your pet is out of pain, and stop hurting yourself with doubt or guilt. You loved this special animal and gave him/her the best you could give. You didn't abandon him when he/she was ill. Appreciate the gifts you gave and the love you offered.

Finally, please know you will get through this rough time. This is a life experience. It deepens your ability to feel compassion and love. Later, you will help others with their losses, and you will understand how they feel. This is the deepest level of connection we humans have. And our animals have given this to us. We must show our gratitude to them for enriching our lives.

I believe animals are our connection to each other. By allowing yourself the time, space and permission to grieve, you become a more balanced human, capable of loving again. And you will.

Marian Silverman is a licensed family therapist and educational psychologist and has been a consultant and animal-assisted therapy specialist for the PAC program at UCLA Medical center.

She can be reached at hollyni@sbcglobal.net

DEAR GOD

Kathy Vusovich

You have tested me again today. It's only been four weeks. My heart hasn't healed yet from losing my baby. Today my Lindy left me. I should think the fact that you have all my other children you would have given me Lindy for a little more time. We needed each other.

I hope she closed her eyes and was greeted by Widget, Amelia and Misty. She has missed Widget this past four weeks. She wandered the house every day checking up on the sofa and on top of the bed. She knew her sister had to be in one of those spots sleeping soundly. When she wandered for days and couldn't find her, she branched out and looked elsewhere. She knew her baby sister wouldn't leave without saying "good-bye". They were inseparable for ten years. They were at my side for ten years.

I was blessed that hot July day when I walked into an antique store and saw those sad brown eyes behind a little fence with a sign saying, "need a good home". When I was told she had been badly abused and the shop owner had just brought her in that morning—I knew we were meant to be together.

We got home and walked into the house to meet Amelia and Misty. They took one look and said, "Mom has brought us another sister". That was that. She was welcomed into safe arms from that moment on. She had a loving mom and sisters that she adored.

Lindy never left my side. If I got off the couch to go to the kitchen, she followed. My days of privacy were over. She sat in the bathroom waiting for me each morning. If I had to go to work, she was sitting on the cold concrete every night waiting and watching through her fence. She let me park my car but as soon as I opened the car door, she bounced and barked to greet me. All the way into the house she was like a pogo stick. How wonderful it was to be so loved by God's creatures.

Tonight will be the first night in twenty years I won't have my pups to tend to. It's the first night I won't have them breathing softly and sleeping soundly. I won't be able to check on them several times before I'm sure they're settled in and I can go to sleep. I don't know what I will do tomorrow when I don't have to get clean bowls and fresh water before I start my day. I don't know what I will do for days and weeks to come. My girls were the loves of my life.

Please God take care of my babies. Please heal the blind eyes, deaf ears and terrible seizures they endured in their precious lives. I know they will be safe and happy if they are all together again.

Please heal the pain in my broken heart.

Heart-Warming Tales

A DOG'S PURPOSE (FROM A 6-YEAR-OLD).

Being a veterinarian, I had been called to examine a ten-year-old Irish Wolfhound named Belker. The dog's owners, Ron, his wife Lisa, and their little boy Shane, were all very attached to Belker, and they were hoping for a miracle.

I examined Belker and found he was dying of cancer. I told the family we couldn't do anything for Belker, and offered to perform the euthanasia procedure for the old dog in their home.

As we made arrangements, Ron and Lisa told me they thought it would be good for six-year-old Shane to observe the procedure. They felt as though Shane might learn something from the experience.

The next day, I felt the familiar catch in my throat as Belker's family surrounded him. Shane seemed so calm, petting the old dog for the last time, that I wondered if he understood what was going on. Within a few minutes, Belker slipped peacefully away.

The little boy seemed to accept Belker's transition without any difficulty or confusion. We sat together for a while after Belker's death, wondering aloud about the sad fact that animal lives are shorter than human lives. Shane, who had been listening quietly, piped up, 'I know why.'

Startled, we all turned to him. What came out of his mouth next stunned me. I'd never heard a more comforting explanation.

He said, "People are born so that they can learn how to live a good life—like loving everybody all the time and being nice, right?" The six-year-old continued, "Well, dogs already know how to do that, so they don't have to stay as long."

It came to me that every time I lose a dog,
they take a piece of my heart with them.
And every new dog who comes into my life,
gifts me with a piece of their heart.
If I live long enough,
all the components of my heart
will be a dog, and I will become
as generous and loving as they are.

—Unknown

THE FOURTH DAY

Martin Scot Kosins

If you ever love an animal, there are three days in your life you will always remember…

The first is a day, blessed with happiness, when you bring home your young new friend.

You may have spent weeks deciding on a breed. You may have asked numerous opinions of many vets, or done long research in finding a breeder. Or, perhaps in a fleeting moment, you may have just chosen that silly looking mutt in a shelter—simply because something in its eyes reached your heart.

But when you bring that chosen pet home, and watch it explore, and claim its special place in your hall or front room—and when you feel it brush against you for the first time—it instills a feeling of pure love you will carry with you through the many years to come.

The second day will occur eight or nine or ten years later.

It will be a day like any other. Routine and unexceptional. But, for a surprising instant, you will look at your longtime friend and see age where you once saw youth.

You will see slow deliberate steps where you once saw energy.

And you will see sleep when you once saw activity.

So you will begin to adjust your friend's diet—and you may add a pill or two to her food.

And you may feel a growing fear deep within yourself, which bodes of a coming emptiness. And you will feel this uneasy feeling, on and off, until the third day finally arrives.

And on this day—if your friend and whatever higher being you believe in have not decided for you, then you will be faced with making a decision of your own—on behalf of your lifelong friend, and with the guidance of your own deepest Spirit.

But whichever way your friend eventually leaves you—you will feel as alone as a single star in the dark night sky.

If you are wise, you will let the tears flow as freely and as often as they must. And if you are typical, you will find that not many in your circle of family or friends will be able to understand your grief, or comfort you.

But if you are true to the love of the pet you cherished through the many joy-filled years, you may find that a soul—a bit smaller in size than your own—seems to walk with you, at times, during the lonely days to come.

And at moments when you least expect anything out of the ordinary to happen, you may feel something brush against your leg—very, very lightly.

And looking down at the place where your dear, perhaps dearest, friend used to lie—you will remember those three significant days.

The memory will most likely to be painful, and leave an ache in your heart.

As time passes the ache will come and go as if it has a life of its own.

You will both reject it and embrace it, and it may confuse you.

If you reject it, it will depress you.

If you embrace it, it will deepen you.

Either way, it will still be an ache.

But there will be, I assure you, a fourth day when—along with the memory of your pet—and piercing through the heaviness in your heart—there will come a realization that belongs only to you.

It will be as unique and strong as our relationship with each animal we have loved, and lost.

This realization takes the form of a Living Love—

Like the heavenly scent of a rose that remains after the petals have wilted, this Love will remain and grow—and be there for us to remember.

It is a love we have earned.

It is the legacy our pets leave us when they go.

And it is a gift we may keep with us as long as we live.

It is a Love which is ours alone.

And until we ourselves leave, perhaps to join our Beloved Pets—

It is a Love we will always possess.

Martin Scot Kosins is the author of *Maya's First Rose*, published by Open Sky Books.

"The Fourth Day" originally appeared as the Foreword for Pet Loss by Nieburg and Fischer, published by HarperPerennial.

Published here with permission of Martin Scot Kosins.

THE STORY OF TANK

They told me the big black Lab's name was Reggie as I looked at him lying in his pen. The shelter was clean, no-kill, and the people really friendly. I'd only been in the area for six months, but everywhere I went in the small college town, people were welcoming and open. Everyone waves when you pass them on the street.

But something was still missing as I attempted to settle in to my new life here, and I thought a dog couldn't hurt. Give me someone to talk to. And I had just seen Reggie's advertisement on the local news. The shelter said they had received numerous calls right after, but they said the people who had come down to see him just didn't look like "Lab people," whatever that meant. They must've thought I did.

But at first, I thought the shelter had misjudged me in giving me Reggie and his things, which consisted of a dog pad, bag of toys almost all of which were brand new tennis balls, his dishes, and a sealed letter from his previous owner. See, Reggie and I didn't really hit it off when we got home.

We struggled for two weeks (which is how long the shelter told me to give him to adjust to his new home). Maybe it was the fact that I was trying to adjust, too. Maybe we were too much alike.

For some reason, his stuff (except for the tennis balls—he wouldn't go anywhere without two stuffed in his mouth) got tossed in with all of my other unpacked boxes. I guess I didn't really think he'd need all his old stuff, that I'd get him new things once he settled in. but it became pretty clear pretty soon that he wasn't going to.

I tried the normal commands the shelter told me he knew, ones like "sit" and "stay" and "come" and "heel," and he'd follow them—when he felt like it. He never really seemed to listen when I called his name—sure, he'd look in my direction after the fourth of fifth time I said it, but then he'd just go back to doing whatever. When I'd ask again, you could almost see him sigh and then grudgingly obey.

This just wasn't going to work. He chewed a couple of shoes and some unpacked boxes. I was a little too stern with him and he resented it, I could tell. The friction got so bad that I couldn't wait for the two weeks to be up, and when it was, I was in full-on search mode for my cell phone amid all of my unpacked stuff. I remembered leaving it on the stack of boxes for the guest room, but I also mumbled, rather cynically, that the "damn dog probably hid it on me."

Finally I found it, but before I could punch up the shelter's number, I also found his pad and other toys from the shelter. I tossed the pad in Reggie's direction and he snuffed it and wagged, some of the most enthusiasm I'd seen since bringing him home. But then I called, "Hey, Reggie, you like that? Come here and I'll give you a treat." Instead, he sort of glanced in my direction—maybe "glared" is more accurate—and then gave a discontented sigh and flopped down. With his back to me.

Well, that's not going to do it either, I thought. And I punched the shelter phone number.

But I hung up when I saw the sealed envelope. I had completely forgotten about that, too. "Okay, Reggie," I said out loud, "let's see if your previous owner has any advice."...

To Whoever Gets My Dog:

Well, I can't say that I'm happy you're reading this, a letter I told the shelter could only be opened by Reggie's new owner. I'm not even happy writing it. If you're reading this, it means I just got back from my last car ride with my Lab after dropping him off at the shelter. He knew something was different. I have packed up his pad and toys before and set them by the back door before a trip, but this time it's like he knew something was wrong. And something is wrong... which is why I have to go to try to make it right.

So let me tell you about my Lab in the hopes that it will help you bond with him and he with you.

First, he loves tennis balls, the more the merrier. Sometimes I think he's part squirrel, the way he hoards them. He usually always has two in his mouth, and he tries to get a third in there. Hasn't done it yet. Doesn't matter where you throw them, he'll bound after it, so be careful—really—don't do it by any roads. I made that mistake once, and it almost cost him dearly

Next, commands. Maybe the shelter staff already told you, but I'll go over them again: Reggie knows the obvious ones—"sit," "stay," "come," "heel." He knows hand signals: "back" to turn around and go back when you put your hand straight up; and "over" if you put your hand out right or left. "Shake" for shaking water off, and "paw" for a high-five. He does "down" when he feels like lying down—I bet you could work on that with him some more. He knows "ball" and "food" and "bone" and "treat" like nobody's business.

I trained Reggie with small food treats. Nothing opens his ears like little pieces of hot dog.

Feeding schedule: twice a day, once about seven in the morning, and again at six in the evening. Regular store-bought stuff; the shelter has the brand, He's up on his shots. Call the clinic on 9th Street and update his info with yours; they'll make sure to send you reminders for when he's due. Be forewarned: Reggie hates the vet. Good luck getting him in the car—I don't know how he knows when it's time to go to the vet, but he knows.

Finally, give him some time. I've never been married, so it's only been Reggie and me for his whole life. He's gone everywhere with me, so please include him on your daily car rides if you can. He sits well in the back seat, and he doesn't bark or complain. He just loves to be around people, and me most especially.

Which means that this transition is going to be hard, with him going to live with someone new.

And that's why I need to share one more bit of info with you…His name's not Reggie.

I don't know what made me do it, but when I dropped him off at the shelter, I told them his name was Reggie. He's a smart dog, he'll get used to it and will respond to it, of that I have no doubt. But I just couldn't bear to give them his real name. For me to do that, it seemed so final, that handing him over to the shelter was as good as me admitting that I'd never see him again. And if I end up coming back, getting him, and tearing up this letter, it means everything's fine. But if someone else is reading it, well…well it means that his new owner should know his real name. It'll help you bond with him. Who knows, maybe you'll even notice a change in his demeanor if he's been giving you problems.

His real name is Tank. Because that is what I drive.

Again, if you're reading this and you're from the area, maybe my name has been on the news. I told the shelter that they couldn't make "Reggie" available for adoption until they received word from my company commander. See, my parents are gone, I have no siblings, no one I could've left Tank with...and it was my only real request of the Army upon my deployment to Iraq, that they make one phone call to the shelter...in the "event"...to tell them that Tank could be put up for adoption. Luckily, my colonel is a dog guy, too, and he knew where my platoon was headed. He said he'd do it personally. And if you're reading this, then he made good on his word.

Well, this letter is getting too downright depressing, even though, frankly, I'm just writing it for my dog. I couldn't imagine if I was writing it for a wife and kids and family. But still, Tank has been my family for the last six years, almost as long as the Army has been my family. And now I hope and pray that you make him part of your family and that he will adjust and come to love you the same way he loved me.

That unconditional love from a dog is what I took with me to Iraq as an inspiration to do something selfless, to protect innocent people from those who would do terrible things...and to keep those terrible people from coming over here. If I had to give up Tank in order to do it, I am glad to have done so. He was my example of service and of love. I hope I honored him by my service to my country and comrades.

All right, that's enough. I deploy this evening and have to drop this letter off at the shelter.

I don't think I'll say another good-bye to Tank, though. I cried too much the first time. Maybe I'll peek in on him and see if he finally got that third tennis ball in his mouth.

Good luck with Tank. Give him a good home, and give him an extra kiss goodnight—every night—from me.

Thank you, Paul Mallory

I folded the letter and slipped it back in the envelope. Sure I had heard of Paul Mallory, everyone in town knew him, even new people like me.

Local kid, killed in Iraq a few months ago and posthumously earning the Silver Star when he gave his life to save three buddies. Flags had been at half-mast all summer.

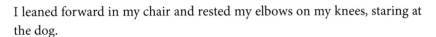

I leaned forward in my chair and rested my elbows on my knees, staring at the dog.

"Hey, Tank," I said quietly.

The dog's head whipped up, his ears cocked and his eyes bright.

"Come here, boy."

He was instantly on his feet, his nails clicking on the hardwood floor. He sat in front of me, his head tilted, searching for the name he hadn't heard in months.

"Tank," I whispered. His tail swished.

I kept whispering his name, over and over, and each time, his ears lowered, his eyes softened, and his posture relaxed as a wave of contentment just seemed to flood him. I stroked his ears, rubbed his shoulders, buried my face into his scruff and hugged him.

"It's me now, Tank, just you and me. Your old pal gave you to me."

Tank reached up and licked my cheek.

"So what do you say we play some ball?

His ears perked again.

"Yeah? Ball? You like that? Ball?"

Tank tore from my hands and disappeared in the next room.

And when he came back, he had three tennis balls in his mouth.

Animals are reliable,
many full of love,
true in their affections,
predictable in their actions,
grateful and loyal.
Difficult standards for
people to live up to.

—Alfred A. Montapert

A MAN'S BEST FRIEND

Senator George Graham Vest, speaking to a jury about his dog,
Old Drum, shot in 1869.

"The best friend man has in the world may turn against him and become his enemy. His son, or daughter, that he has reared with loving care, may prove ungrateful. Those who are nearest and dearest to us, those whom we trust with our happiness and good name may become traitors to their faith. The money a man has he may lose. It flies away from him, perhaps when he needs it most. A man's reputation may be sacrificed in a moment of ill-considered action. The people who are prone to fall on their knees when success is with us may be the first to throw the stone of malice when failure settles its cloud upon our head.

The one absolutely unselfish friend that man can have in this selfish world, the one that never deserts him, the one that never proves ungrateful or treacherous, is his dog. A man's dog stands by him in prosperity and poverty, in health and in sickness. He will sleep on the cold ground when the wintry winds blow and the snow drives fiercely, if only to be near his master's side. He will kiss the hand that has no food to offer, he will lick the wounds and sores that come in encounters with the roughness of the world. He guards the sleep of his pauper master as if he were a prince.

When all other friends desert, he remains. When riches take wing, and reputation falls to pieces, he is as constant in his love as the sun in its journey through the heavens.

If fortune drives his master forth, an outcast in the world, friendless and homeless, the faithful dog asks no higher privilege than that of accompanying him, to guard him against danger, to fight against his enemies. And when that last scene of all comes, and death takes his master in its embrace and his body is laid away in the cold ground, no matter if all other friends pursue their way, there, by the graveside will the noble dog be found, his head between his paws, his eyes sad, but open in alert watchfulness, faithful and true, even in death."

I have developed a deep respect for animals.
I consider them fellow living creatures
with certain rights that should not be
violated any more than those of humans.

—*Jimmy Stewart*

A PET'S 10 COMMANDMENTS

1. My life is likely to last 10–15 years. Any separation from you is likely to be painful.

2. Give me time to understand what you want of me.

3. Place your trust in me. It is crucial for my well-being.

4. Don't be angry with me for long and don't lock me up as punishment. You have your work, your friends, your entertainment, but I have only you.

5. Talk to me. Even if I don't understand your words, I do understand your voice when speaking to me.

6. Be aware that however you treat me, I will never forget it.

7. Before you hit me, before you strike me, remember that I could hurt you, and yet, I choose not to bite you.

8. Before you scold me for being lazy or uncooperative, ask yourself if something might be bothering me. Perhaps I'm not getting the right food, I have been in the sun too long, or my heart might be getting old or weak.

9. Please take care of me when I grow old. You too, will grow old.

10. On the ultimate difficult journey, go with me please. Never say you can't bear to watch. Don't make me face this alone. Everything is easier for me if you are there, because I love you so.

Take a moment today to thank God for your pets. Enjoy and take good care of them.

Life would be a much duller, less joyful experience without God's critters

We do not have to wait for Heaven, to be surrounded by hope, love, and joyfulness.

It is here on earth and has four legs!

LIKE ALL THE OTHER KIDS

by Laura Kelley

My first Schnauzer, Syd, had been owned by a family with kids before he came into my life.

At age 8, he got lost and somehow ended up running into my downtown office. When I finally found out who his owners were, they told me they didn't want him back, saying he didn't like their small kids.

I had no children, and was delighted to have such a sweet little dog. I soon found out there had been some parts of living with children that Syd had liked, though. One afternoon while out for a walk, he began pulling me as hard as he could, which was unusual for gentle little Syd. I let him lead, and he would turn right at one corner, left at another, and clearly had some purpose.

I never connected his behavior with the distant jingle of ice cream truck music until we turned down the street it was on, and he made a bee line for it. I bought him a popsicle, and he was delighted. Eventually the ice cream truck started coming through our apartment complex's driveway. Syd always heard it in plenty of time to let me know, so I could get my money ready and his leash on, and we'd go out and line up with all the other "kids" to get his popsicle. He seemed to have no idea he wasn't one of them. The children thought it was hysterical and would offer him a lick of theirs, to the horror of their parents. In the aftermath, other moms would be wiping sticky little hands and faces, and I'd be wiping Syd's beard.

In time, I adopted two more Schnauzers and bought a house. The others learned the routine from him, and I'd have three little bearded faces pressed against the fence when the familiar refrains sounded through the streets of our new neighborhood. Since he was my first, I always let him be the one to go out to the street with me to get the treat to be shared. This was our afternoon routine for the next nine summers.

Syd died at the age of 17, in late September, after the ice cream truck season had ended.

The first time the ice cream truck jingled down the street the next spring, I reflexively reached into my pocket, praying I had the cash to get Syd his ice cream. Then I sat down on the steps and sobbed when it hit me that he wasn't there. In a neighborhood of mainly older folks and young, as-yet childless couples, the ice cream trucks must not do well. Their popsicles are overpriced, often freezer-burned. Some of the neighbors complain about the volume of the music and the speeds at which they drive. But that tinny music warms my heart, because I can see Syd sitting at the door, eagerly waiting to line up for his afternoon treat with all the other kids.

WHERE TO BURY A DOG

by Ben Hur Lampman (1886–1954)

There are various places within which a dog may be buried. We are thinking now of a setter, whose coat was flame in the sunshine, and who, so far as we are aware, never entertained a mean or an unworthy thought. This setter is buried beneath a cherry tree, under four feet of garden loam, and at its proper season, the cherry strews petals on the green lawn of his grave. Beneath a cherry tree, or an apple, or any flowering shrub of the garden, is an excellent place to bury a good dog. Beneath such trees, such shrubs, he slept in the drowsy summer, or gnawed at a flavorous bone, or lifted head to challenge some strange intruder. These are good places, in life or in death. Yet it is a small matter, and it touches sentiment more than anything else.

For if the dog be well remembered, if sometimes he leaps through your dreams actual as in life, eyes kindling, questing, asking, laughing, begging, it matters not at all where that dog sleeps at long and at last. On a hill where the wind is unrebuked and the trees are roaring, or beside a stream he knew in puppyhood, or somewhere in the flatness of a pasture land, where most exhilarating cattle graze. It is all one to the dog, and all one to you, and nothing is gained, and nothing lost—if memory lives. But there is one best place to bury a dog. One place that is best of all.

If you bury him in this spot, the secret of which you must already have, he will come to you when you call—come to you over the grim, dim frontiers of death, and down the well-remembered path, and to your side again. And though you call a dozen living dogs to heel they should not growl at him, nor resent his coming, for he is yours and he belongs there.

People may scoff at you, who see no lightest blade of grass bent by his footfall, who hear no whimper pitched too fine for mere audition, people who may never really have had a dog. Smile at them then, for you shall know something that is hidden from them, and which is well worth the knowing.

The one best place to bury a good dog is in the heart of his master.

Comforting
Poems

All the arguments to prove man's superiority cannot shatter this hard fact: in suffering, the animals are our equals.

—Pete Singer

SAYING GOODBYE

Attributed to Susan A. Jackson

May I go now? Do you think the time is right?
May I say good-bye to the pain filled days and nights?
I've lived my life and done my best…as a good friend tried to be.
So can I take that step beyond and set my spirit free?

I didn't want to go at first. I fought it with all my might.
But something seems to draw me now to a warm and loving light.
I want to go. I really do. It's difficult to stay.
But I will try as best I can to live Just One More Day.

To give you time to care for me and share your love and fears.
I know you're sad and are afraid, because I see your tears.
I'll not be far, I promise you, I hope you'll always know
That my spirit will be close to you wherever you go.

Thank you for loving me. You know I love you too…
That's why it is so hard to say good-bye and end this life with you.
So hold me now, just one more time and let me hear you say…
Because you care so much for me you'll let me go today

FROM FRIEND TO FRIEND
Author unknown

You're giving me a special gift,
So sorrowfully endowed,
And through these last few cherished days,
Your courage makes me proud.

But really, love is knowing
When your best friend is in pain,
And understanding earthly acts
Will only be in vain.

So looking deep into your eyes,
Beyond, into your soul,
I see in you the magic, that will
Once more make me whole.

The strength that you possess,
Is why I look to you today,
To do this thing that must be done,
For it's the only way.

That strength is why I've followed you,
And chose you as my friend,
And why I've loved you all these years...
My partner 'til the end.

Please, understand just what this gift,
You're giving, means to me,

It gives me back the strength I've lost,
And all my dignity.

You take a stand on my behalf,
For that is what friends do.
And know that what you do is right,
For I believe it too.

So one last time, I breathe your scent,
And through your hand I feel,
The courage that's within you,
To now grant me this appeal.

Cut the bonds that hold me here,
Dear friend, and let me run,
Once more a strong and steady dog,
My pain and struggle done.

And don't despair my passing,
For I won't be far away,
Forever here, within your heart,
And memory I'll stay.

I'll be there watching over you,
Your forever friend,
And in your memories I'll play,
A young dog once again.

WAITING AT THE GATE

Author Unknown

I explained to St. Peter
I'd rather stay here
Just outside the Pearly Gate.
I won't be a nuisance, I won't even bark,
I'll be very patient and wait.

I'll be right here chewing
A celestial bone
No matter how long you may be.
'Cause I'd miss you too much,
If I went in alone.
It wouldn't be heaven for me.

*Children and dogs are as necessary
to the welfare of the country as
Wall Street and the railroads.*

—*Harry S. Truman*

VELICITY

Your loving owner Kristen Repoli, age 10

Your death was unexpected,
Memories fill my mind,
As soft as a cloud,
As small as a rabbit
You brighten my mood,
You will always be in my heart,
Your death causes my pain,
Your playfulness was my gain,
You'll always be remembered,
You'll always be my dog
You aren't suffering any more
You are in a better place
I can imagine you on a white fluffy cloud
Chasing butterflies,
Prancing around,
Looking down on me,
Smiling

TRIBUTE TO A BEST FRIEND

Author Unknown

Sunlight streams through the window pane onto a spot on the floor…
then I remember,
it's where you used to lie, but now you are no more.
Our feet walk down a hall of carpet, and muted echoes sound…
then I remember,
it's where your paws would joyously abound.
A voice is heard along the road, and up beyond the hill,
then I remember,
it can't be yours…your golden voice is still.
But I'll take that vacant spot of floor and empty muted hall,
and lay them with the absent voice and unused dish along the wall.
I'll wrap these treasured memories in a blanket of my love,
and keep them for my best friend until we meet above.

*One cannot look deeply into the
eyes of an animal and not see the
same depth, complexity and feeling
we humans lay exclusive claim to.*

—Nan Sea Love

CREATION

Author Unknown

When God had made the earth and sky,
the flowers and the trees,
He then made all the animals
the fish, the birds and bees
And when at last He'd finished
not one was quite the same.
He said I'll walk this world of mine
and give each one a name.
And so He travelled far and wide
and everywhere He went,
a little creature followed Him
until its strength was spent.
When all were named upon the earth
and in the Sky and Sea,
the little creature said "Dear Lord,
there's no name left for me."
Kindly the Father said to him
"I've left you to the end.
I've turned my own name back to front
And called you DOG, my friend".

INSCRIPTION ON THE MONUMENT
OF A NEWFOUNDLAND DOG.

A Memorial to Boatswain
by Lord Byron
Newstead Abbey, November 30, 1808.

Near this spot
Are deposited the Remains of one
Who possessed Beauty without Vanity,
Strength without Insolence,
Courage without Ferocity,
And all the Virtues of Man without his Vices.
This Praise, which would be unmeaning Flattery
If inscribed over human ashes,
Is but a just tribute to the Memory of
BOATSWAIN, a DOG
Who was born at Newfoundland, May, 1803,
And died at Newstead, Nov 18th, 1808

When some proud son of man returns to earth,
Unknown to glory, but upheld by birth,
The sculptor's art exhausts the pomp of woe,
And storied urns record who rest below:
When all is done, upon the tomb is seen,
Not what he was, but what he should have been:
But the poor dog, in life the firmest friend,
The first to welcome, foremost to defend,

Whose honest heart is still his master's own,
Who labours, fights, lives, breathes for him alone,
Unhonour'd falls, unnoticed all his worth,
Denied in heaven the soul he held on earth:
While man, vain insect! hopes to be forgiven,
And claims himself a sole exclusive heaven.
Oh man! thou feeble tenant of an hour,
Debased by slavery, or corrupt by power,
Who knows thee well must quit thee with disgust,
Degraded mass of animated dust!
Thy love is lust, thy friendship all a cheat,
Thy smiles hypocrisy, thy words deceit!
By nature vile, ennobled but by name,
Each kindred brute might bid thee blush for shame.
Ye! who perchance behold this simple urn,
Pass on —it honours none you wish to mourn:
To mark a friend's remains these stones arise;
I never knew but one, —and here he lies.

A DOGGIE PRAYER

Author Unknown

Do not grieve for me, my friend,
as I am with my kind.

My collar is a rainbow's hue
My leash a shooting star
My boundaries are the milky way
Where I sparkle from afar.

There are no pens or kennels here
For I am not confined
But free to roam God's heavens
Among my special kind.

I nap the day on a snowy cloud
With gentle breezes rocking me
I dream the dreams of earthlings
And how it used to be.

The trees are full of liver treats
And tennis balls abound
And milk bones line the walking ways
Just waiting to be found.

There even is a ring set up
The grass all lush and green
And everyone who gaits around
Becomes the "Best Of Breed".

For we're all winners in this place

We have no faults you see
And God passes out the ribbons
To each one—even me.

At night I sleep in angels' arms
Their wings protecting me
And moonbeams dance about us
As stardust falls on thee.

So when your life on earth is spent
And you reach heaven's gate
Have no fear of loneliness
For here, you know I wait.

DO NOT MOURN MY PASSING

Author Unknown

Do not mourn my passing
for if you could only see
by slipping all my earthly bonds,
I'm young again and free.
By day I run the Heavenly fields,
my body healthy and strong.
At night I sleep at Angels' Feet,
lulled by Celestial Song.
So do not mourn my passing,
just close your eyes—you'll see.
I'm once again that frisky pup,
just as you remember me.

*We must protect the forests for our children,
grandchildren, and children yet to be born.
We must protect the forests for those who
cannot speak for themselves such as
the birds, animals, fish and trees.*

—Chief Qwatsinas

THE LAST BATTLE

Author Unknown

If it should be that I grow frail and weak
And pain should keep me from my sleep,
Then will you do what must be done,
For this…the last battle…can't be won.

You will be sad I understand,
But don't let grief then stay your hand,
For on this day, more than the rest,
Your love and friendship must stand the test.

We have had so many happy years,
You wouldn't want me to suffer so.
When the time comes, please, let me go.

Take me to where to my needs they'll tend,
Only, stay with me till the end
And hold me firm and speak to me
Until my eyes no longer see.
I know in time you will agree
It is a kindness you do to me.

Although my tail its last has waved,
From pain and suffering I have been saved.
Don't grieve that it must be you
Who has to decide this thing to do;

We've been so close…we two…these years,
Don't let your heart hold any tears.

LAST NIGHT

Author unknown

I stood by your bed last night;
I came to have a peep.
I could see that you were crying
And you found it hard to sleep.

I whined to you softly
As you brushed away a tear,
"It's me, I haven't left you,
I'm well, I'm fine, I'm here."

I was close to you at breakfast,
I watched you pour the tea,
You were thinking of the many times,
Your hands reached down to me.

I was with you at the shops today;
Your arms were getting sore.
I longed to take your parcels;
I wish I could do more.

I was with you at my grave today;
You tend it with such care.
I want to re-assure you,
That I'm not lying there.

I walked with you towards the house,
As you fumbled for your key.
I gently put my paw on you;

I smiled and said, "It's me."

You looked so very tired,
And sank into a chair.
I tried so hard to let you know,
That I was standing there.

It's wonderful for me, to be
So near you every day.
To say to you with certainty,
"I never went away."

You sat there very quietly,
Then smiled, I think you knew...
In the stillness of that evening,
I was very close to you.

The day is over...
I smile and watch you yawning
and say "good-night, God bless,
I'll see you in the morning."

And when the time is right for you
To cross the brief divide,
I'll rush across to greet you
And we'll stand, side by side.

I have so many things to show you,
There is so much for you to see.
Be patient, live your journey out...
Then come home to be with me.

DON'T GRIEVE FOR ME

Author Unknown

Don't grieve for me, for now I am free.
I'm following paths God made for me
I took his hand, I heard him call...
Then turned, and bid farewell to all.
I could not stay another day
To laugh, to love, to sing, to play.
Tasks left undone must stay that way
I found my peace...at close of day.
And if my parting left a void
Then fill it with remembered joy.
A friendship shared, a laugh, a kiss,
Ah yes, these things I too will miss.
Be not burdened...deep with sorrow,
I wish you sunshine of tomorrow.
My life's been full...I've savored much.
Good friends, good times...a loved one's touch
Perhaps my time seemed all too brief.
Don't lengthen it now with undue grief.
Lift up your heart and share with me,
God wants me now...He set me free!

FREE NOW

Author Unknown

Free now to run and jump and play
Or snooze in the shade on a sunny day.
To sit for hours watching birds in the trees
Or to lie on the porch and enjoy the breeze.

Free from the sickness that made me so weak,
Restored to the dog that I was at my peak.
You made the right choice for me, my friend.
Be at ease with yourself and let your heart mend.

No more vets, no shots, not even a pill.
And while you can't see me, I'm here with you still.
For though you may think that we really did part
I'm there in your memories, I'm here in your heart.

*An animal's eyes have the power
to speak a great language.*

—*Martin Buber*

I ONLY WANTED YOU

Author Unknown

They say memories are golden
Well maybe that is true.
I never wanted memories,
I only wanted you.

A million times I needed you,
A million times I cried.
If love alone could have saved you
You never would have died.

In life I loved you dearly,
In death I love you still.
In my heart you hold a place
No one could ever fill.

If tears could build a stairway
And heartache make a lane,
I'd walk the path to heaven
And bring you back again.

Our family chain is broken,
And nothing seems the same.
But as God calls us one by one,
The chain will link again.

AN OWNER'S PLEA

Author Unknown

Please, God, if You should hear a scratch on Eden's Gate tonight,
A gentle whine, a muffled bark; have Peter take a light
And open up the Pearly Gates and call her Spirit in,
For I think she lived in Heaven once; please take her back again.
She may have been a mongrel, without a pedigree,
Yet she was noble, kind and good; I think You will agree:
That she'll be very useful where the souls of children play.
She'll romp with them, and see, Dear God, they do not go astray.
Just tell her that we're sorry that we could not pat her head,
And whisper how we loved here 'ere her Spirit fled.
I pray that when death beckons, and my soul surmounts life's fog,
I'll rate a place in Heaven, Dear God, beside our dog.

My little dog—
a heartbeat at my feet.

—Edith Wharton

A POEM FOR THE GRIEVING

Author Unknown

Do not stand at my grave and weep.
I am not there, I do not sleep.
I am a thousand winds that blow,
I am the diamond glints on snow.
I am the sunlight on ripened grain,
I am the gentle autumn's rain.
When you awaken in the morning's hush,
of quiet birds in circled flight.
I am the stars that shine at night.
Do not stand at my grave and cry,
I am not there, I did not die...

NOTE: There is considerable conflict over the actual authorship of this poem. It is most commonly attributed to a Mary Frye (and believed to have been written around 1932); however, nothing is known of the author. It is, however, believed to be one of the most requested (and reprinted) poems in the English language!

PUT ME TO REST

Author Unknown

Time to let me go my friend,
Because my life no-one can mend,
It's better to let me go this way,
Than watch me suffer night and day.

I'm happy to go, my time has come,
My quality of life is no longer fun,
I've been so ill, so it's not a bad thing,
To let me go forever resting.

Stay with me till I drift away,
Fast asleep forever I pray,
To relieve me from suffering and pain,
What more can I ask from my best friend.

Don't be sad, I'll be free from pain,
Never to be ill ever again,
I know you'll miss me being there,
But all the memories you have to share.

Thank you for being my best friend,
And all my needs that you did tend,
Try not to be sad, try not to cry,
Now is the time to say goodbye
Put me to rest.

When people tell me they cannot stand losing a pet

I tell them that the joy they bring us in life

Far outweighs the grief we feel when they die.

That joy is great indeed,

And I wouldn't miss it for the world.

—*Polly Barnes*

AS LONG AS FOREVER

Author Unknown

As long as Forever
I will stay by your side
I'll be your companion,
Your friend and your guide.

As long as I live
And as long as you care,
I'll do anything for you,
I'll go anywhere.

I'll bring you the sunshine,
I'll comfort your fears,
I'll gather up rainbows
To chase all your tears.

As long as forever
My heart will be true.
For as long as I live,
I'll always love you.

A DOG'S PRAYER
TO THOSE WHO LOVE & THOSE WHO LOVE ME

Author Unknown

When I am gone, release me, let me go—
I have so many things to see and do.
You must not tie yourself to me with tears,
Be happy that we had so many years.
I gave you my love, you can only guess
How much you gave me in happiness.
I thank you for the love you have each shown.
But now it is time I traveled alone.
So grieve awhile for me if grieve you must,
Then let your grief be comforted by trust,
It is only for a while that we must part,
So bless the memories within your heart,
I will not be far away, for life goes on,
So if you need me, call and I will come.
Though you cannot see or touch me, I will be near.
And if you listen with your heart, you will hear
All my love around you soft and clear.
And then, when you must come this way alone,
I will greet you with a smile and "Welcome Home".

If you pick up a starving dog and make him prosperous, he will not bite you. This is the principal difference between a dog and a man.

—*Mark Twain*

HAVE YOU A DOG IN HEAVEN?

Author Unknown

Have you a dog in Heaven, Lord?
And do you pat its head?
Does he sit up and beg each night
Before he goes to bed?
Does he look up with shining eyes
when he sees Your smiling face?
Does he wag his stubby little tail
When he wants to run a race?
Have You a dog in Heaven, Lord?
Is there room for just one more?
Cause my little dog died today;
He'll be waiting at Your door.
Please take him into Heaven, Lord.
And keep him there for me,
Just feed him, pet him, love him, Lord,
That's all he'll ask of Thee.

FOR ALL THE JOYS

Author Unknown

I will lend to you for awhile
a puppy, God said,
For you to love him while he lives
and to mourn for him when he is gone.
Maybe for twelve or fourteen years,
or maybe for two or three
But will you, till I call him back
take care of him for me?

He'll bring his charms to gladden you
and (should his stay be brief)
you'll always have his memories
as solace for your grief.
I cannot promise that he will stay,
since all from earth return,
But there are lessons taught below
I want this pup to learn.

I've looked the whole world over
in search of teachers true
And from the folk that crowd life's land
I have chosen you.
Now will you give him all your love
Nor think the labor vain
Nor hate me when I come to take my pup back again.

I fancied that I heard them say
"Dear Lord Thy Will Be Done,"
For all the joys this pup will bring,
the risk of grief you'll run.
Will you shelter him with tenderness
Will you love him while you may
And for the happiness you'll know forever grateful stay.

But should I call him back
much sooner than you've planned
Please brave the bitter grief that comes
and try to understand.
If, by your love, you've managed
my wishes to achieve,
In memory of him that you've loved,
cherish every moment with your faithful bundle,
and know he loved you too.

My
Dogster
Diary

When I was at my lowest point during Abby's final months, and needed support the most, I stumbled across the "Dogster" website. I found a community, 500,000 strong, of the most loving, supportive and caring pet owners that I could have ever imagined.

When I had questions, they had answers; when I cried, they had virtual tissues; when I needed TLC, they had virtual hugs. When it was Abby's time to go, they were there with support, empathy, consolation, and loving "wings" to comfort me.

Dogster Rocks!

MY DOGSTER DIARY

Counting Down the Days
July 26th, 12:12 pm

It's now just over 5 months since we took Abby to the vet to have her limp looked at. (We thought it was a pinched nerve). The vet called us right back and said come back in immediately. The x-rays showed osteosarcoma in the right front leg. The vet said it was highly malignant and she could put Abby to sleep right away. We said "No Way, Not Today!" and we've had a wonderful time together since. She's slowing down and licking both paws now quite a bit, but she still has that waggy tail, and she still wants to play with the squeaky toys. How do we know when it's time?

Day By Day
August 1st, 11:13 am

We saw the vet again yesterday, and she said that she was amazed that Abby is still with us five months later. She thought maybe two months. We are so glad that she is still with us. She's licking her paws a lot and the vet says that that is an indication of pain. We don't want her to be in pain or to suffer. Yet she seems so full of life. She wags her tail like crazy when she sees us in the morning. She has a great appetite (though Cushing's disease plays a part in that). She is continent and regular and she can walk herself. And she wants to play with her squeaker toys. So how do we know when it's time? How do we know that it's US being selfish and wanting one more day?

Just One More Day
August 15th, 11:54 am

Well, here we are at the middle of the month, and that's almost 6 months since D-Day (diagnosis day!). I treasure every new day with Abby, and I'm noticing how easy it is for me now to let the tears flow at the thought of losing her. Maybe if I get all the tears out now, there won't be any left later, and it won't be so painful. She's definitely slowing down, but still wants to play, and still can walk outside herself. Her eyes do look a little sadder though. Just One More Day…please…

And the Days Dwindle Down
August 29th, 10:14 am

I just heard that Clive's beautiful Wheaton Terrier Simon crossed over the Rainbow Bridge yesterday and my heart is heavy. So many people have to face this loss every day, have to make the decision to call the vet every day,—it's so sad. But the joy our pets give us, it so totally outweighs the eventual grief.

Abby is still with us. Every morning her tail wags as I give her the first morning tummy rub. We're spoiling her rotten with treats and she's shedding a lot now (more so than usual), but she still has a good appetite, can walk outside and just Loves her new squeaky toy. So we're enjoying every precious day with her.

Just One More Day…Please.

Wow, we're on Doggie Cloud Nine!
September 2nd, 1:23 am

Dogster just named Abby—"Dog of the Day". What a Huge Honor! Abby's tail hasn't stopped wagging since I told her. This just really lifts our spirits, especially since Abby's time is drawing to a close. It's now September and our vet, who is a really wonderful, compassionate lady, didn't think Abby would stay around past April. It's amazing what lots of love and tummy rubs can do. We still don't know really How to Tell When It's Time. We're just going day by day. Lots of people tell us that Abby will let us know with her eyes. Right now her eyes just say "More Food, Please".

I'm now half way through writing a book on knowing when it's time. It's going to be a "Chicken Soup" type book, and so if anyone has stories on how THEY knew it was time, and would like to share, please write me at geoff@azuradawn.com

I'd love to include all the stories I can. Thanks for reading the diary, and thanks everyone for all the support.

Your Support Touches our Heart.
September 7th, 11:32 pm

Wow, we have been overwhelmed with letters of support, Pup Pal requests, Rosettes, Stars and all kinds of Gifts and Comments. This is just so wonderful. This support is exactly what we needed, and is so much appreciated. What a wonderful community this is. There is so much Love going around here. Can't thank you all enough. I want to answer everyone.

Abby has Cushing's as well as osteosarcoma, so she's always hungry and thirsty, and obviously spends a lot more time wanting to go take care of business. The good thing is that she still can do it all on her own. (If anyone has a dog with Cushing's and wants more info, I have an over 100 page-book that I will be happy to share. It was very informative, and has good holistic remedies.)

Abby still wants to play her favorite game which is "Try to Take My Squeaky Toy Outta My Mouth If You Can"—and we never can 'cos she's tooo quick for us. She still tries to stuff 2 tennis balls in her mouth at one time, and she still plays waggy tail like crazy. I don't think it's time yet, but her eyes are definitely losing the sparkle she once had. "Just One More Day"…please.

Autumn Leaves start to fall
September 23rd, 2:07 pm

…and our Vet is amazed that Abby is still with us. She's a fighter! She's licking her paws a lot more, which is the standard sign of pain, so my wife and I are having more and more discussions on when it's time. No-one wants to cause pain to their pet, and we all want as much time with them as we can. Gosh, this is so difficult, and yet, it is so wonderful to see her each morning, just a-wagging that tail like crazy. Her appetite is great, she can walk outside to poop, so we're taking each day at a time, and being so thankful for it. Just One More Day, oh pleez, oh pleez.

Counting Down The Days
October 7th, 5:16 pm

We're getting close to having to call the Vet in. (We've decided that we want Abby to cross the Bridge here at home). She's licking her paws a lot more, her right front paw is swollen with a tumor (the original tumor was on her left paw), she's drinking like there's a drought (from the Cushing's)and she's limping noticeably. We increased her Zubrin anti-inflammatory to 2 x 200mg tablets to help with the pain.

Yet she can still walk herself out to poop, still has an appetite and still wants to play. The research I've done seems to come down to—Is she having more good days than bad days? Well,—we don't want her to have bad days. We don't want her to suffer. And our biggest fear is that her leg will break and cause her needless pain. The good thing is that she still wants and loves her tummy rubs, still plays with her squeakers and still wants to try and stuff 3 tennis balls into her mouth. (Still can do only 2 !).

Is it crazy that I'm crying and she's still here?

Isn't the crying supposed to be after she's gone?

I guess I know the time's coming…and that's why I'm determined to make sure that she goes just surrounded with oodles of love. The Dogster support is just awesome. It helps so much. We're waiting for her to tell us when.

Just One More Day…please.

Oh Gosh, Not Today!
October 11th, 10:22 am

I took Abby out this morning to poop, she pooped and then she just sort of put her butt down on the sidewalk and vegged out. That was unusual. Especially with the Cushing's, food / breakfast is All Important. After about 5 minutes, she got up and came in for her food. I gave her the Zubrin medication (2 tablets instead of the 1-1/2 that we'd given her before). She took the meds and then breakfast. She ate it all, which indicated good appetite. But then, she was very itchy on both sides, and agitated, just walking around, following me everywhere, licking rubbing scratching. That was a few hours ago, and she's calmed down a bit now, but Dawn, my wife, says that it's time. She said that Abby told her last night. Of course, I'm asking for one more day. "It's Sunday, the Vet is not available". We've had lots of tears, and we're just going to see how the day goes.

It's All About The Love
October 12th, 8:35 am

Yesterday was freaky. Abby probably got a bite on her nose from either a spider or a wasp, 'cos it swelled up later and she was trying to rub it all the time. I knew something was very wrong by her agitation. She calmed down later in the day. However, we realize that the decision has to be made soon. She has a couple of big tumors near her neck, she has tumors in her front paws, she itches her haunches a lot and she wheezes a bit now. We now the cancer progresses, yet she can walk out side, she has a good appetite still and she still rolls over for her tummy rubs. The tough part is that she really can't tell us just how much pain she is in. We're getting close, but I now understand so much of what I've read in other Diaries. Everyone wants Just One More Day. My task is to realize that loving her is also about letting her go. That's so hard.

A Wake Up Call From The Vet
October 20th, 12:58 am

I called the vet today to find out what we should do if something happened with Abby at night or on the weekend. The vet called back later to give us her cell phone number and also to give us a prescription for a sedative, if we couldn't reach her. She said that with Abby's cancer, six months after diagnosis was the maximum that she had ever seen because the cancer spreads so rapidly. (Abby is now 8 months past the diagnosis). The vet also said that the constant licking means that Abby is definitely in pain. That's what is so hard for me to understand. When Abby and our cat Spunky would play together, Spunky used to bat Abby on her nose and sometimes nicked her with a claw. Abby would squeal a bit. That to me was pain being expressed. Now, there is no sound. How can that mean she is in pain? The vet suggested very gently to us that we decide on a date and give her 48 hours notice. She also said that Abby's appetite probably would never go away because of her Cushing's disease. I have been thinking that the appetite meant she was still OK. I haven't seen Abby tell me that it's time yet. Is she staying on because she knows we don't want to let her go? Just One More Day

Coming Up on Her Halloween Barkday.
October 27th, 6:08 pm

Abby is still with us, and her Barkday is almost here—All Hallows Eve.. She'll be 13. Abby is still so alert, so present, so adorable—we just can't think of calling the Vet in. As long as she can walk, poop, eat, play and enjoy tummy rubs, and lick my broken foot to heal me. We're not there yet for the vet call. I'm recovering from fractured heel surgery, and we limp outside together when she has to go, and I'm not ready to be put down yet, so we're hangin' in there for AbberDabbers—and we treasure each and every day.

Can it really be NOW?
November 20th, 8:14 am

I feel so guilty because I've been rubbing Abby's tummy and her tailing is wagging madly and the tears are streaming down my face, and I know we're at the time to make THE decision. She's been limping badly for a few days, and we really don't want her to suffer, and we really don't want her to go, and it really is time, and we don't want to make the decision, and we don't want her to suffer. Oh, Dear it's so hard. We're going to call the vet later this morning. The support from Dogster Pals has been awesome. Thanks.

Just One More Day
November 21st, 9:09 am

We cried and we thought and we cried and we thought and then we decided that since Abby can poop by herself and has a great appetite, and just loves her new Purple Platypus squeaky toy—Then maybe, just maybe, it's not quite time yet. Everyone says she will tell us with her eyes, and she's just not saying that right now. She's saying—"Where's my food" and "Let's play Ball". So, we're going to wait until Monday to make the decision. And we're going to surround her with oodles of love .

The Time Has Come
November 25th, 7:39 pm

Well, we made an appointment with the Vet to come here on Friday at Noon. Abby's legs crumbled last night when she went to pee, and then she really didn't want to go back up the two small steps into the house. We haven't seen "the look in the eyes", that people talked about, but Dawn (Abby's Mom) says she knows it's time. We can see the tumor breaking through her front leg, it's obviously very weak, and we definitely don't want her to cross the Bridge with a broken leg.

We've had a wonderful extra nine months that the Vet is just amazed about. It seems so crazy that we're crying so much before she's even gone. She's so alert and playful. The Vet said that we can change our mind, right up to the last minute. This is so tough a decision to make. I wonder if there are pet owners who feel that this is a decision they shouldn't make and they just let nature take it's course, despite the pain? For us, we are sure that we don't want her to suffer, and we're sure that this will be an act of supreme love. We just keep wanting "Just One More Day".

We Can Change Our Mind If We Want To!
November 27th, 6:22 pm

We just couldn't do it! The Vet told us that when they took Abby away today, her body would just lay on a cold slab until Monday, and that wasn't something we wanted to happen, so we told the vet to make it Monday. We woke up and were feeling pretty numb to begin with, and then the reality sunk in, and we were just both bawling, and trying to comfort each other and reason out the situation—Pro's and Con's.—" She's limping, so she must be in pain"; But she's got a good appetite, and she's pooping regularly" She's had highly malignant cancer for over 9 months now"—But she's so playful and full of life" and we went back and forth and then finally we couldn't bear to think of her on a cold slab over the weekend, so we cancelled today's appointment.

But Abby still got ham omelet for breakfast!—She loved it.

Today's the Day
November 30th, 10:46 am

It's 10:30am and the Vet will be here at noon. We know this is the right decision, but it still doesn't stop me from hoping the vet will have some kind of other emergency and won't be able to make it.

We were up super early and gave Abby a wonderful hamburger and scrambled eggs with her dry food. She loved it. She's been Miss Waggy Tail all morning. Everyone has been so supportive. Dawn's at peace with our decision, but we've both been streaming tears all morning. I'm going now—back to the tummy rubs :-)

Abby's At The Bridge
November 30th, 4:17 pm

Quite simply, this was the hardest thing we have ever had to do. We spent the whole morning just lavishing lots of love on Abby, big breakfast, lots of strokes and tummy rubs. Secretly, I was hoping that the Vet would not be able to make it. However, she was there at Noon. She validated for us that this was the best for Abby that the cancer was just traveling throughout her body and this was the supreme act of love from us. She was amazed that Abby had lasted so long—it's wonderful what the Power of Love can do. We know we did the right thing, but that didn't make it any easier. And it was over so quickly. That was probably for the best.

Now Abby is wagging her tail at all her new friends on Rainbow Bridge.

My friend Polly has given me some wonderful words of comfort. She said:

"When people tell me they cannot stand losing a pet, I tell them that the Joy they bring us in life Far outweighs the grief we feel when they die. That Joy is great indeed, and I wouldn't miss it for the world."

It has also been comforting to have the support of all our Dogster Pals— More than anything, they have helped us through this with their Love and Caring and Compassion:—Zaidie, Zoei, Simon's Dad Clive, Wyoming Cheyenne and Debbie, Augie, Autumn Angel & Mom, Austin & LouAnn, JoJo Jolanda & Mom, Riley, Miss Honey Pie's Family, The Lafayette Little Rascals, Roxxie, Tater Tots, Gigi, Cherish, Kirby, Tasha, Geordie, Teddy and Layla, Tyler, K.C's Family, Blackie Angel Baby, Checkers, Doo, Girl Dog ExtraOrdinair, bobbi E + The Wolf House, Saphira + Family, Jet, Tramp,

Rascal, Crystal, Mr. Barney "Paws", Kappa, Tucker Blu, Maggie Mouse, Coco and the Whole Caring Dogster Family. Love To You All

OOPS, I Missed a Whole Bunch of Thank-Yous
November 30th, 4:48 pm

AND…

Quindred Spirit + Family; Buddy; Sandy Rascal +Angel Whiskey; Amber; Bailey; Angel Tutti; Winnie Joy; Raven + Family; Paco Kimber + Squeaker; Raoudi; Zoe + Cece; Cocoa + Rudie; Zoee + Chloee; Blackwell + Lexi; Tessa + Fitzcairn; NINJA;

Thank you ALL for such wonderful Warmth and Loving. I can't tell you enough how much it gave us the will to handle the sadness. God Bless You.

You Tube Video Link for Abby
November 30th, 4:57 pm

Here's a link to a video that Dawn put together. Hope you like it.

Enjoy.

http://www.youtube.com/watch?v=2faziAXqdJ4#watch-main-area

The Tears Flow Freely
December 8th, 2:09 am

I picked up Abby's ashes this evening from the Vet's office. On the way back home, I opened the window on the passenger side 'cos Abby always loved to put her nose out and let the wind just rush all over her face. When she got diagnosed with the osteosarcoma, the Vet said it wouldn't be good to take Abby for walks anymore, because it would put too much pressure on her leg (front), so I used to take her for a drive in the car every day. I guess this was our last drive together.

I know she's found lots of new friends at The Rainbow Bridge and I know she's not in pain anymore. And we miss her so much. There's no-one to bark when someone is at the front door, and there's no waggy tail in the mornings. And there's so many tears—I don't know where they all come from.

I haven't been able to go to Dogster until today, but I saw so many wonderful messages and so much love and support. It really does mean so much to us. Thank you.

Head in the Sand
February 13th, 12:56 am

I'm slowly realizing that I've been putting my head in the sand for the past 6 or 7 weeks. Playing ostrich. I didn't want to cry anymore. It hurt too much. So I just went numb. Occasionally, the tears would come flying out, like someone opened the flood gates, but I managed to close them quickly.

I realize that I wasn't grieving, I was stopping myself from grieving.

I didn't put up the "Abby with Wings" images that Autumn and Putter and Hunter's pawrents had so lovingly made for us. I didn't want to go to Dogster, because then I'd have to think about Abby and cry some more. I didn't want to write a single word more for my book, 'cos it was too painful.

I forgot that tears are cleansing, that they need to come out, and that they will come out sooner or later (sometimes when you least expect them).

We miss you AbberDabbers,—you're forever in our hearts, and we know that you have oodles of Dogster pals to play with at The Rainbow Bridge.

We've started barking whenever the doorbell rings, in your memory, girl.

Thanks to all our Dogster friends for their loving support. We proudly display "Abby with Wings". Thanks Autumn, Thanks Putter, Thanks Hunter. I hope we can give back love and support just like all the love we've received. And I hope I've learned that crying is Good!

Rescue
Dogs

THE DOG WE RESCUED ACTUALLY SAVED US

By: Margot Vincent

Our black lab passed away several months ago. Each member of the family coped with her death in a different way. My youngest son acted out, becoming aggressive and uncharacteristically grumpy. I suffered in silence, figuring that the best way for all of us to "get over" the death was for me to remain a pillar of strength.

We decided that although we would never forget Borrie, we would get a lab puppy during the summer. As a teacher, I would have the time and energy to train a puppy during my time off.

This idea was greeted with nothing but skepticism from practically everyone I knew, as they reminded me, that I was expecting a baby and I would be certifiable to try to take on a new baby and a new puppy at the same time.

The more I thought about it, the more I agreed with them. Superwoman I am not. However, I knew we had to get a dog back into our lives. Our house was not the same without one.

This is when we began to consider adopting an older dog. Our neighbor told us about a place called Joyful Rescues, and she suggested that I check out the Web site. Tentatively, I accessed the site. I slowly read, "Each Joyful Rescues pet has been thrown away at least once and/or lived a horrific life so far."

There were about 40 dogs available for adoption. I scanned the list and looked at the photos. About three-fourths of the way down the page, I stopped. There was a white dog whose eyes were captivating. She seemed to be smiling at me. She was a young, medium sized, white German shepherd mix.

Her story was amazing. She was described as "sweet to a fault, wonderful with other dogs, cats [which we have] and kids of all ages [which we also have]." She had severely broken her leg. The break was too bad to repair. Because of this, her right hind leg had been amputated.

The Web site went on to say that after this happened, "her spirit and carefree ways never wavered. She was fine getting around and there was no shortage of kisses for anyone."

I froze. This sounded like the perfect dog. We needed copious kisses.

My family agreed that we should meet her. On a sunny Saturday morning, we piled into the car and drove an hour and a half to see her. During the trip, my husband and I reviewed with the kids how to act when meeting a new dog. We reminded them to let the dog come to them, and to not put their faces near her face.

Upon arriving, we walked up the driveway with great excitement and apprehension. Then it happened. She came to us immediately, rolled on her back, wagged her tail and licked everyone. She was clearly saying, "My family is finally here. What took you so long?"

My heart danced. My husband winked and nodded. The dog could not have been more relaxed. Destiny.

We spent an hour visiting with her, but we needed only that first minute to know that she was our new dog. My youngest son, who hadn't smiled in what seemed like forever, was giddy. We didn't need an adorable, tiny puppy. We needed Kaia as much as she needed us.

When we finally had her home, one day she looked up as if to say, "How will I ever thank you?"

Little does she know that we are the lucky ones. We may have rescued her, but she actually rescued us.

First published in the Buffalo News. Reprinted with permission of author.

I RESCUED A HUMAN TODAY

By: Janine Allen

Her eyes met mine as she walked down the corridor peering apprehensively into the kennels. I felt her need instantly and knew I had to help her.

I wagged my tail, not too exuberantly, so she wouldn't be afraid. As she stopped at my kennel I blocked her view from a little accident I had in the back of my cage. I didn't want her to know that I hadn't been walked today. Sometimes the overworked shelter keepers get too busy and I didn't want her to think poorly of them.

As she read my kennel card I hoped that she wouldn't feel sad about my past. I only have the future to look forward to and want to make a difference in someone's life.

She got down on her knees and made little kissy sounds at me. I shoved my shoulder and side of my head up against the bars to comfort her. Gentle fingertips caressed my neck; she was desperate for companionship. A tear fell down her cheek and I raised my paw to assure her that all would be well.

Soon my kennel door opened and her smile was so bright that I instantly jumped into her arms.

I would promise to keep her safe. I would promise to always be by her side.

I would promise to do everything I could to see that radiant smile and sparkle in her eyes.

I was so fortunate that she came down my corridor. So many more are out there who haven't walked the corridors. So many more to be saved. At least I could save one.

I rescued a human today.

http://rescuemedog.org/dog-blog/i-rescued-a-human-today-by-janine-allen/

Written by Janine Allen CPDT, Rescue Me Dog's professional dog trainer. Janine's passion is working with people and their dogs. She provides demonstrations for those who have adopted shelter dogs, lends email support to adopted dog owners that need information beyond our Training Support Pages, and aids shelter staff and volunteers in understanding dog behavior to increase their adoptability. Copyright 2011 Rescue Me Dog; www.rescuemedog.org

Animals can communicate quite well.
And they do.
And generally speaking, they are ignored.

—*Alice Walker*

TOP 10 REASONS TO VISIT A SHELTER

🐾 Great place to recycle your towels and bedding.

🐾 It's Free.

🐾 Experience the abundance and variety of a dog show.

🐾 You'll be the center of attention.

🐾 Discover new opportunities to help sharing the experience such as volunteering.

🐾 It gives you something to talk about.

🐾 You can find a friend or two.

🐾 Find a personal trainer that will work for treats.

🐾 Save a life.

🐾 Fall in love

TOP 10 REASONS TO ADOPT A SHELTER DOG

- 🐾 One less dog will remain in the shelter.

- 🐾 You might find a purebred at a fraction of the price.

- 🐾 You can adopt an exotic breed, like a Bali Temple Dog, without leaving the Country.

- 🐾 Gives you a reason to call all your friends and family.

- 🐾 Babe/Dude magnet—We are talking model quality.

- 🐾 You don't have to worry about any fooling around and making puppies.

- 🐾 A good reason to go out for a walk.

- 🐾 Someone to talk to.

- 🐾 Teaches commitment without joining the military.

- 🐾 A good reason to go straight home.

Fun
Stuff

DOG RULES

1. The dog is NOT allowed in the house.

2. Okay, the dog is allowed in the house, but ONLY in certain rooms.

3. The dog is allowed in all rooms, but has to stay OFF the furniture.

4. The dog can get on the OLD furniture only.

5. Fine, the dog is allowed on all the furniture, but is not allowed to sleep with the humans on the bed.

6. Okay, the dog is allowed on the bed, but only by invitation.

7. The dog can sleep on the bed whenever he wants, but not under the covers.

8. The dog can sleep under the covers by invitation only.

9. The dog can sleep under the covers every night.

10. Humans must ask permission to sleep under the covers with the dog

If you think dogs can't count,
try putting three biscuits in your pocket
and then give him only two of them.

—Phil Pastoret

MY TRIP TO THE GROCERY STORE

Yesterday, I was at my local store buying a large bag of dog chow for my loyal pet, Biscuit, the Wonder Dog. I was in the checkout line when the woman behind me asked if I had a dog.

What did she think I had, an elephant? So, since I'm retired and have little to do, on impulse I told her that no, I didn't have a dog, I was starting the "Dog Food Diet" again. I added that I probably shouldn't, because I ended up in the hospital last time, but that I'd lost 50 pounds before I awakened in an intensive care ward with tubes coming out of most of my orifices and IVs in both arms.

I told her that it was essentially a perfect diet, and that the way that it works is to load your pants' pockets with doggy nuggets and simply eat one or two every time you feel hungry. The food is nutritionally complete, so it works well and I was going to try it again. (I have to mention here that practically everyone in line was now enthralled with my story.)

Horrified, she asked if I ended up in intensive care because the dog food poisoned me.

I told her no, I stepped off a curb to sniff an Irish Setter's butt, and a car hit us both.

I thought the guy behind her was going to have a heart attack, he was laughing so hard.

The store won't let me shop there anymore. Better watch what you ask retired people. They have all the time in the world to think of crazy things to say.

WHY DOGS ARE BETTER THAN MEN

Author Unknown

Dogs do not have problems expressing affection in public.

Dogs miss you when you're gone.

You never wonder whether your dog is good enough for you.

Dogs feel guilt when they've done something wrong.

Dogs don't brag about whom they have slept with.

Dogs don't criticize your friends.

Dogs admit when they're jealous.

Dogs do not play games with you—except fetch (and then never laugh at how you throw).

Dogs are happy with any video you choose to rent, (because they know the most important thing is that you're together).

Dogs don't feel threatened by your intelligence.

You can train a dog.

Dogs are already in touch with their inner puppies.

You are never suspicious of your dog's dreams.

Gorgeous dogs don't know they're gorgeous.

The worst social disease you can get from dogs is fleas. (OK, the "really" worst disease you can get from them is rabies, but there's a vaccine for it, and you get to kill the one that gives it to you.)

Dogs understand what "no" means.

Dogs don't need therapy to undo their bad socialization.

Dogs don't make a practice of killing their own species.

Dogs understand if some of their friends cannot come inside.

Dogs think you are a culinary genius.

You can house train a dog.

You can force a dog to take a bath.

Dogs don't correct your stories.

Middle-aged dogs don't feel the need to abandon you for a younger owner.

Dogs aren't threatened by a woman with short hair.

Dogs aren't threatened by two women with short hair.

Dogs don't mind if you do all the driving.

Dogs don't step on the imaginary brake.

Dogs admit it when they're lost.

Dogs don't weigh down your purse with their stuff.

Dogs do not care whether or not you shave your legs.

Dogs take care of their own needs.

Dogs aren't threatened if you earn more than they do.

Dogs mean it when they kiss you.

Dogs are nice to your relatives.

WHY DOGS ARE BETTER THAN WOMEN

Author unknown

Dogs don't cry.

Dogs love it when your friends come over.

A dog's time in the bathroom is limited to quick drinks.

The later you are, the more excited a dog is to see you.

Dogs will forgive you for playing with other dogs.

Dogs don't notice (or care) if you call them by another dog's name.

Dogs can appreciate excessive body hair.

Anyone can get a good-looking dog.

Dogs like when you leave lots of things on the floor.

Dogs never need to examine the relationship.

Dogs understand that instincts are better than asking for directions.

Dogs understand that all animals smaller than dogs were made to be hunted.

Dogs like beer.

No dog ever bought a Kenny G, Cher, or Barbara Streisand album.

Dogs agree you have to raise your voice to get your point across.

It's legal to keep a dog chained up at your house.

Dogs find you amusing when you're drunk.

Dogs can't talk.

*Did you ever notice when you
blow in a dog's face, he gets mad at you?
But when you take him in a car,
he sticks his face out the window!*

—Steve Bluestone

WHO IS YOUR REAL FRIEND?

This really works!

If you don't belive it, just try this experiment.

Put your dog and your spouse in the trunk of the car for an hour. When you open the trunk, which one is really happy to see you?

THE 10 MOST POPULAR
DOG BREEDS IN THE UNITED STATES

According to the American Kennel Club, the most popular
breeds for the past 10 years are as follows:

	RANKING			
	2011	**2010**	**2006**	**2001**
BREED				
Labrador Retrievers	1	1	1	1
German Shepherd Dogs	2	2	3	3
Beagles	3	4	5	5
Golden Retrievers	4	5	4	2
Yorkshire Terriers	5	3	2	6
Bulldogs	6	6	12	19
Boxers	7	7	7	8
Poodles	8	9	8	7
Dachshunds	9	8	6	4
Rottweilers	10	11	17	11

Being patted is what it's all about.

—*Roger Caras*

It's
a Dog's
Life

DOG OCCUPATIONS

Military War Dogs (MWD) www.uswardogs.org

Military Working Dogs have been used by the U.S. Military since World War I. American families donated their dogs to the military to aid our troops during wartime. Dogs, along with their volunteer handlers, trained in teams as scouts, trackers, sentry, mine/booby-trap/tunnel and water detection of hostile forces. Dogs were used in WWI, WWII, Korea, Vietnam, Persian Gulf, Bosnia, Kosovo, Afghanistan and Iraq. It has been estimated that these courageous canine heroes saved over 10,000 lives during the conflict in Vietnam.

Today all branches of our Armed Forces are utilizing Military Patrol Dogs specializing in Drug and Bomb/Explosive detection. There are approximately 600–700 of these canines in the Middle East in such places as Kuwait, Afghanistan, Saudi Arabia and Iraq. They are being used to patrol Air Bases, Military Compounds, Ammunition Depots and Military Check Points. They are guarding and protecting our Military Personnel as they were trained to do, with Courage, Loyalty and Honor.

Therapy Dogs

The use of therapy dogs is continuously rising in popularity. They must show a love and warmth for all people. They are frequently used in hospitals and nursing homes, and provide great companionship. They raise patients' spirits and have been shown to lower blood pressure. Golden Retrievers are often used due to their calm demeanor, gentle disposition and friendliness to strangers.

Rescue Dogs

There are two types of rescue dogs—Air scenting and Trailing/Tracking dogs. Air-scenting dogs use airborne human scent to hone in on a subject, and they are trained for avalanche and rubble searches and also as cadaver dogs. German and Belgian shepherds or Golden / Labrador retrievers are mostly used in search and rescue situations. In Europe, the St. Bernard dog was bred for rescue in the Italian and Swiss Alps, and although no longer used for alpine rescues, they saved many lives over the years.

Trailing and Tracking dogs are used to search for a specific person after they have been given their scent. Mostly they are German shepherds, Dobermans and Bloodhounds because of their adaptability to different terrains.

Service / Assistance Dogs

Mobility assistance dogs are trained to help physically disabled people. They can pick up objects, open and close doors, operate light switches, pull wheelchairs, and act as "walker" dogs for people with Parkinson's disease.

Seeing-eye dogs are trained to lead visually impaired or blind people around obstacles. The most popular breeds for this type of guide dog are Golden retrievers, Labradors, German shepherds and Labradoodles.

Hearing dogs are specifically selected to assist the deaf and hearing impaired by alerting them to important sounds such as doorbells, smoke alarms, ringing telephone and alarm clocks.

Detection Dogs

Dogs have been trained to search for many substances, including agricultural items and plants for Customs services. A dog's sense of smell has been measured as 10,000 to 100,000 times superior to a human's.

They also are being used for medical purposes, and from urine samples, can detect prostate cancers, as well as cancers of the skin, lung and bladder.

The Pine Street Foundation of San Anselmo, California is doing groundbreaking research on canine scent detection. One study involved five canines who had been taught to recognize lung and breast cancer from human breath samples. They were able to correctly spot breast cancer 88% of the time and lung cancer with 99% accuracy.

In England, the Oxon Support Group for Cancer and Bio-Detection Dogs is training dogs to use their noses to help cancer research scientists, and to assist people with potentially fatal health conditions such as hypoglycemia and Addisonian crisis. Their research shows that about 70% of dogs naturally detect the scent of such conditions as epilepsy and diabetes, and only need to be trained to react properly. Their FaceBook page is "Cancer and Bio-Detection Dogs.

Bed Bug Sniffing Beagles

Bergdorf Goodman, a NYC Department store has hired a bunch of beagles (bevy of beagles?) that have been specifically trained to sniff out bed bugs. There are a couple of companies now in the business of finding bed bugs in hospitals, nursing homes, apartments, homes, stores—using dogs. One of the dogs, Roscoe, even has his own FaceBook page (Bed Bug Dog Roscoe).

Police Dogs (K-9's)

Traditionally, a police dog is used to enforce public order by chasing and holding suspects. The most common breeds used are German Shepherds and Belgian Malinois. Also Bloodhounds are used for search and rescue, and Beagles for drug and explosive detection.

Resources

*There is no psychiatrist in the world
like a puppy licking your face.*

—Ben Williams

PET LOSS SUPPORT TELEPHONE HELPLINES:

- **Arizona:** Companion Animal Association of Arizona. 602-995-5885. 24-hour information line about resources in Arizona, and nationwide links. www.caaainc.org

- **ASPCA National Pet Loss Helpline:** 1-877-474-3310. Free nationwide consultation to bereaved animal owners on a 24-hour basis. (If your call is answered with a recording, please speak clearly, leave your own name and telephone number, and your call will be returned as soon as possible.)

- **California:** University of California at Davis staffs the pet loss support hotline, Monday through Friday, from 6:30 pm–9:30 pm (PST). The phone number is 530-752-4200 / 800-565-1526 or you can access pet loss information through www.vetmed.ucdavis.edu/petloss/index.htm.

- **Nikki Hospice Foundation for Pets** (NHFP) Pet Loss Support Hotline, Vallejo, Ca. 707-557-8595. Callers are invited to leave a brief message if no one answers, and carefully articulate their name and call-back number, especially if using a cell phone or when emotionally distressed, so that messages do not become garbled or unintelligible. Calls will be returned as quickly as possible, usually within 72 hours.

- **Delta Society Pet Loss Support Hotline**, Palm Springs, CA 619-320-3298

- **Colorado:** Colorado State University—970-297-1242 (M–F, 9-5 MT)

- **Florida:** 352-294-4430 University of Florida Veterinary Medical Center Pet Loss Support Hotline; www.vetmed.ufl.edu/patientcare/petlosssupport/

- **Illinois:** 217-244-2273 or toll-free 877-394-2273(CARE). Staffed by University of Illinois veterinary students. Sunday, Tuesday and Thursday evenings 7–9 pm (CST); www.cvm.uiuc.edu/CARE/

- **Chicago:** 630-325-1600 Staffed by Chicago VMA veterinarians and staff. Leave voice-mail message; calls will be returned 7 pm to 9 pm (CST). www.chicagovma.org/petlosssupport/

- **Indiana:** Pet Loss Support Group—(317) 898-1051 (Colleen)

- **Iowa:** Iowa State University Toll-free Pet-Loss Support Hotline 1-888-478-7574 (toll-free) Hours of operation: September–April: 7 days a week, 6:00–9:00 pm (CST).

  May–August: Monday, Wednesday, Friday, 6:00–9:00 pm (CST).

- **Maryland–Virginia–DC:** 540-231-8038 Staffed by Regional College of Veterinary Medicine; Tuesday, Thursday, 6pm–9 pm (ET)

- **Massachusetts:** 508-839-7966 Staffed by Tufts University veterinary students; Monday through Friday, 6 pm to 9 pm (ET); voice-mail messages will be returned daily, collect outside Massachusetts; http://www.tufts.edu/vet/petloss/

- **Michigan:** Michigan State University College of Veterinary Medicine. 517-432-2696 Staffed by Michigan State University veterinary students; Tuesday to Thursday, 6:30 pm to 9:30 pm (ET); http://cvm.msu.edu/alumni-friends/information-for-animal-owners/pet-loss-support/pet-loss-support-hotline/

- **Minnesota:** Social Work Services, University of Minnesota Veterinary Medical Center—612-624-9372.

- **New Jersey:** CONTACT of Burlington County, NJ. 856-234-4688. Offers free telephone support, information and referrals to anyone who is mourning or anticipating the loss of a pet; 24-hour crisis helpline.

- **New York:** Cornell University Pet Loss Support Hotline—607-253-3932, Tuesday–Thursday, 6–9 pm (ET). However, for the summer month of August, the hotline is only available on Wednesday from 6–9 pm (but messages can be left and will still be returned) .

  www.vet.cornell.edu/public/petloss (In addition to information about the hotline itself, this site lists other hotlines and offers several useful articles on loss, grieving, euthanasia and more).

- **New York City:** The Animal Medical Center. 212-838-8100

- **Ohio:** 614-292-1823 Staffed by The Ohio State University veterinary students; Monday through Friday, 6:30 pm to 9:30 pm (ET), and Saturday and Sunday, 10 am to 4 pm (ET); voice-mail messages will be returned collect, during operating hours; http://www.vet.ohio-state.edu/honoringthebond.htm

- **Oregon:** Dove Lewis Emergency Animal Hospital Pet Loss Support Services. 24-hour message line 503-234-2061 (Long distance calls will be returned collect). E-mails can be sent to grief counselor, Director of Pet Loss Support Services, Enid Traisman, MSW at etjournl@teleport.com. www.dovelewis.org·

- **Pennsylvania:** The University of Pennsylvania School of Veterinary Medicine, Philadelphia, 215-898-4529

- **Tennessee:** University of Tennessee College of Veterinary Medicine support line. Monday–Friday, 9am–6pm. 865-755-8839

- **Washington:** 509-335-5704 or toll-free 866-266-8635, Pet Loss Hotline, Washington State University, College of Veterinary Medicine, http://www.vetmed.wsu.edu/plhl/ ; staffed during the semester on Monday, Tuesday, Wednesday, and Thursday 6:30–9:00 pm, and Saturday 1:00-3:00 pm (PST).

- **The Iams Company's Pet Loss Support Center & Hotline**, 1-888-332-7738. A special toll-free number for grieving pet owners, Monday through Friday, 8 am to 5 pm.

- **Association for Pet Loss and Bereavement**. An association of pet loss counselors and professionals. The site offers links, articles, a bookstore, and directories of counselors and pet loss support groups. www.aplb.org

- **Argus Institute for Families and Veterinary Medicine** www.argusinstitute.colostate.edu/

- **Dogster: A community of pet owners who care**. Join Forums, Groups, ask questions, make your own pet profile page, with over 500,000 members. www.dogster.com

Now I lay them down to sleep

The silent days run so deep;

They are no longer filled with pain,

Pure Love in my heart will forever remain.

Amen.

—*Dawn Bain*

Happy Tails to you,

Until we meet again.